Nature in East Norfolk

Peter Allard
Michael Bean
Tony Brown
Ken Rivett
Brian Wooden

Published by
Great Yarmouth Naturalists' Society

First U.K. Edition published in 2000 by Great Yarmouth Naturalists' Society

Text Copyright © 2000 by Peter Allard, Michael Bean, Tony Brown, Ken Rivett and Brian Wooden
Illustrations copyright © 2000 by Pat Nicholls

All rights reserved. No part of this book may be used or reproduced in any manner whatsoever without prior written permission by the authors

ISBN 0-9539361-0-4

Designed and printed by Rondor Printing Co., Lorne Park Road, Lowestoft, Suffolk NR33 0RD

This book is dedicated to the aims of the
Great Yarmouth Naturalists' Society

*"to promote a public awareness of natural history
and the encouragement of its study"*

Black Redstart

Foreword
by Professor David Bellamy

I don't know how many other Natural Historians gained their early inspiration from sailing on the Broads, but I am one of them. What is more, it was reading Arthur Ransome's Coot Club and Big Six, that sowed the seeds of a lifetime of campaigns, to save the worlds wilder places. Here, in this, "head just above water", "Kingdom of Canute", History both natural and people made, are inseparable. Working in symbiosis, Marsh Men and Mother Nature have created this extra special living landscape.

The Broads, are but a chain of medieval peat diggings, sites of industrial dereliction, their wetlands people made and people managed. Vibrant green corridors that have led millions of holidaymakers to discover the secrets of Great Yarmouth, jewel of a National Park in the making. All this and East Norfolk's vibrant coastline, her estuary, heathlands and where the hand of management, hasn't succeeded in holding back the processes of natural succession, rare scraps of woodland. All have inspired local people to become Natural Historians, many of great note.

This is their story. Read all about it and be sure to add this little book, to your Green Renaissance Library.

My sincere congratulations to all the contributors and all the members of the Great Yarmouth Naturalists' Society for crafting this book and so of upholding their long tradition of "promoting public awareness of natural history and the encouragement of its study".

DAVID BELLAMY
BEDBURN
September 2000

Contents

Great Yarmouth Naturalists' Society i

About This Book iii

Part 1   General Introduction
        Chapter 1   The Area Described 1
        Chapter 2   Some Past Local Naturalists 3
        Chapter 3   Designated Places Within Our Area 7

Part 2   The Flora and Fauna in their Setting
        Chapter 1   Woodlands 9
        Chapter 2   Marshlands 23
        Chapter 3   Estuary 34
        Chapter 4   Towns and Villages 40
        Chapter 5   The Coast and Sea-shore 49
        Chapter 6   Inland Freshwater 55
        Chapter 7   Farmland 64
        Chapter 8   Lowland Heath 74
        Chapter 9   A Miscellany of Nature 81

Part 3   An Alphabetical Index of the Flora and Fauna and the Habitats in which they may be found
        Section 1   Plants 91
        Section 2   Trees and Shrubs 95
        Section 3   Birds 96
        Section 4   Mammals 103
        Section 5   Insects
                              - Butterflies 104
                              - Moths 105
                              - Dragonflies and Damselflies 106
                              - Other Insects 107
        Section 6   Spiders 109
        Section 7   Reptiles and Amphibians 109
        Section 8   Fishes 110
        Section 9   Fungi 110

List of Photographs 113

Suggested Further Reading 115

Acknowledgements 117

The Authors 118

Great Yarmouth Naturalists' Society

Over the past 200 years Yarmouth has been the hunting ground for many leading field naturalists. It was inevitable that at some stage they should organise themselves into a group and when our present Society was formed it became the third such organisation the town had seen.

An unofficial grouping had centred on Dawson Turner, the banker, at his Hall Quay premises in the early 1800's but the first formal association was begun in 1889; the founding meeting being held on August 28th at the Free Library. J. E. Knights was treasurer and J. B. Beckett the honorary secretary, and subscriptions were set at half-a-crown (12½p) per annum. This group, however, became defunct during the winter of 1891/1892.

Yet the need for a society existed and, following correspondence in the Yarmouth Mercury, a local branch of the Norfolk and Norwich Naturalists' Society was formed in June 1893. Among its officers were F. Danby Palmer, who acted as vice-chairman and treasurer, and the eminent naturalist Arthur Patterson who was honorary secretary.

Despite this wealth of talent the society went the way of its predecessor and organised nature study was without a base until 1927. In that year a young Ted Ellis spoke to the Rotary Club at Arnold's Restaurant on "Some Delights of a Young Naturalist". At that meeting Dr. H. R. Mayo asked how it was that there was no Great Yarmouth Naturalists' Society. That earnest enquiry led to the first public meeting, on November 23rd 1927, of the third and present Society.

That Meeting was held at Alpha House, Northgate Street, owned by the local historian Harry B. Johnson. Officers were elected and the first president was Dr. Mayo with H. E. Hurrell, the eminent microscopist as chairman, Arthur Patterson as vice-chairman and Messrs Drummond and Ellis joint secretaries. The annual subscription was again half-a-crown and at the first meeting proper on December 14th, one Mrs. Corlett was the first paid-up member. These early gatherings were interspersed with refreshments and music.

The first ramble was held on May 31st 1928, with a trip from Belton to St. Olaves being led by Arthur Patterson. A group of members followed this route almost exactly 50 years later as part of the Society's Golden Jubilee celebration; they were led by Ted Ellis who had taken part in that pioneering excursion.

Black Redstart

With a growing membership the Society's meetings moved to the Town Hall and then the Hospital School. In 1933 Major A. Buxton gave a lecture on "Broadland Birds" using "moving films".

The Society found it difficult to carry on during the Second World War with Mr. Hallam Ashley's talk on "Geology and Scenery" on March 28th 1940 being the last until after hostilities.

With peacetime came the resumption of the Society's activities and the first meeting saw Mr. R. Gaze speaking on "Norfolk Birds".

In the 1960's the Society involved itself in conservation issues and was instrumental, in 1968, in the establishment of Breydon Water as a local nature reserve. Members continued to serve on the Reserve's management bodies until very recently. In 1989 it celebrated 100 years of organised natural history in the town.

The present Society meets at the Central Library fortnightly throughout the winter months and makes several field trips to local, and not so local, places of interest during the summer. Members and non-members are always welcome at the meetings and on the field trips, when there is always something to interest the new or experienced naturalist.

The Society is always interested in receiving any reports of the rare or unusual, or indeed any sighting records, and will always do its best to answer queries on any facet of natural history.

Despite peoples changing habits and lifestyle the Great Yarmouth Naturalists' Society continues to flourish in the spirit of its founders.

About This Book

Welcome to "Nature in East Norfolk". This book follows, somewhat distantly, in the steps of the pioneering work of Charles and James Paget entitled "A Sketch of The Natural History of Yarmouth". It is not intended to be a definitive work on the flora and fauna of Yarmouth, but rather, an easily read and hopefully informative collection of local wildlife records. These records are those of the members of the Great Yarmouth Naturalists' Society, and its friends, which have been made in recent years.

These are records of popular and visible wildlife, the wildlife that each and every one of us is familiar with, the plants and creatures of everyday life. There is mention of rarities, the recording of which has given great pleasure to the recorder, but given the right circumstances, this is a record of the wildlife in the Yarmouth area that any interested observer armed with a field guide can find.

Narrative styles will differ slightly throughout the book as this is the composite work of several writers sharing their interest and expertise with you, the reader, and each has brought his own identity to the project.

We, the Great Yarmouth Naturalists' Society, hope that you will gain much enjoyment from reading this book, and that it may inspire you to take to the open air of town and country to discover the delights of our local natural history at first hand.

The book is divided into 3 main parts.

Part 1 sets the scene by introducing the area covered by this book and the habitats that it contains. It continues with a short history of some past local naturalists and outlines their specialities and tells of their influence on the local study of natural history. There then follows a brief explanation of some of the terminology used when talking of land usage and habitat such as Ramsar Site or Site of Special Scientific Interest.

Part 2 is written in descriptive style and contains chapters on the main habitats of the area and the wildlife to be found therein. Within each chapter is a section on each wildlife group, thus locating each species in a specific habitat. It is not intended that the species discussed in these sections will be the complete list, but a guide to those more commonly found in a particular place. e.g. in order to avoid repetition a plant such as the Annual Meadow Grass *Poa annua* may not be mentioned in all of the habitats in which it has been recorded. Depending upon the likelihood of sightings in a particular habitat some chapters will have the insects sub-divided into sections (e.g. butterflies) to assist location within the book.

The final chapter in this section contains a miscellany of the unusual, of creatures out of their natural habitat and of specialist areas such as molluscs and spiders.

Part 3 contains alphabetical lists of all the species discussed in part 2, along with a key to indicate all the habitats in which they can reasonably be expected to be seen. The numbers in the key correspond to those of the habitat list (chapter numbers) in the preceding section. Using this section will ensure that you have all the habitat locations for a particular species.

Part 1
A General Introduction

Chapter 1 — The Area Described

Yarmouth lies near the most easterly point in the British Isles. The town is situated on a sandbank, which formed at the mouth of an estuary around AD700. The formation of the spit and the subsequent silting up of what now is Breydon Water has helped shape the topography of the area covered by this book.

To the north of Yarmouth lies the Fleggs - an area once an island. To the south are the villages of Lothingland and at the west, the once-extensive marshlands.

Much of the area is encompassed by Broadland, which means that while enjoying a large degree of protection, its wildlife and landscape is also subjected to huge pressures from tourism and recreational interests.

On the relatively higher ground the soils are loamy and intensively farmed, but the lower ground is alluvial and sometimes marshy; here cattle and sheep are reared.

The climate of East Anglia is often described as continental and is characterised by low rainfall.

The coast, in many places has succumbed to holiday developments. But there are fine sandy beaches at Yarmouth and Caister, and dune systems, notably at Winterton and North Yarmouth; sand cliffs are a feature of California and Gorleston. However, parts of the coast are being seriously eroded and considerable effort and expense is being directed at these areas to contain the threat.

The conurbation of Yarmouth and Gorleston, with Bradwell, Belton and Caister, is the largest residential and commercial area. The last twenty years has seen a significant expansion outward, with the subsequent loss of farmland, grassland and dyke systems.

The encroachment on the countryside has been felt also in the larger villages of Hemsby, Ormesby, Martham, Rollesby, Burgh Castle and Hopton. In addition, improvements to the road network have signalled the loss of other wildlife sites.

Within the towns and villages havens for wildlife can be found in private gardens, parks and cemeteries and churchyards. The latter provide sanctuary for many species of flora and fauna, whose existence is otherwise threatened by modern agricultural practices.

Woodland is scarce. There are small wooded areas fringing the Broads and a few isolated marsh carrs with the characteristic species of Alder and Willow, but the largest area is at Fritton. The Waveney Forest, as it is often called, is mainly coniferous and was planted after World War Two. Within its boundaries can be found some of the remnants of the heathland that ran south from Belton and St. Olaves in bygone days.

Stretches of inland freshwater exist in the Broads namely those of Martham, Ormesby, Rollesby and Filby, and at Fritton Decoy and Lound Waterworks. The Rivers Bure, Yare and Waveney enter Breydon Water. Over the years the waterways have become heavily polluted by both agricultural and domestic waste. With the introduction of Government and European legislation and the efforts of the Broads Authority, water quality is beginning to improve in the rivers and Broads.

Another problem though, is the erosion of the riverbanks by increasing holiday traffic. Speed restrictions are often difficult to enforce and so the problem shows little sign of being resolved.

Of all the habitats described in the book, the most significant in size and importance is Breydon Water and the adjoining marshes. This low-lying area has dominated the agriculture of East Norfolk, provided home to a rich diversity of plant and animal life, supplied a livelihood for a unique breed of people who eked out an existence here and added to the geographical and economic isolation of Yarmouth.

Moreover, in recent years, it was the battleground of one of the most important conservation issues of our times. As a result of the fight to save Halvergate Marshes legislation was passed to pay farmers to set aside land of wildlife and landscape value.

Chapter 2 — Some Past Local Naturalists

Yarmouth enjoys a tradition of producing excellent field naturalists. In the 18th century the scene was populated by sportsmen / collectors who shot first and identified second. This fashion continued well into Victorian times but the 19th century also saw a blooming of interest in botany, entomology and geology, led by the burgeoning middle classes. Collecting was gradually replaced by recording for its own sake and, with the arrival of the 20th century, the working classes began taking an interest in the natural world. This trend was also reflected in the formation of natural history societies and Yarmouth has seen three.

Why the area should have favoured so much interest is obvious. The Yarmouth naturalist has been blessed with an exciting variety of habitats. On the doorstep is the relic estuary of Breydon Water, which over the years has produced arguably more rare birds per acre than any region in Britain. The surrounding marshes and dykes have been abundant reservoirs of insects and microscopic life, and the lure of Broadland nearby has been like a magnet that has drawn the most eminent naturalists of their day.

Charles Stuart Girdlestone is perhaps the most interesting of the line of sportsmen / naturalists who were active locally in the 18th and early 19th centuries. Born in 1798, the son of a local physician, Girdlestone began collecting in his teens. By his mid-twenties he was shooting at Hickling and Horsey with the famed Col. Peter Hawker and Richard Lubbock, the Norfolk naturalist. He corresponded with several of the leading naturalists of his day, including the ornithologist P. J. Selby. But Girdlestone was not simply a shooter of birds, he also made astute observations of wildlife and significantly, began a diary he called the 'Game Bag', while a student at Cambridge in 1820. From his contemporaries we know the diary was a most valuable record of the birdlife in East Norfolk. Regrettably its whereabouts is not known it seems to have vanished sometime in the 19th century, though it may have been destroyed when the Tolhouse was bombed in 1941. Girdlestone died of heart failure at the age of 33 years.

Lilly Wigg was born in Smallburgh on Christmas Day, 1749. His father was a shoemaker and brought up his son to follow him in his footsteps. However, before his 20th birthday, Lilly moved to Yarmouth where he opened a school in Row 25, 'Fighting Cock Row'. Despite his humble beginnings he had a knowledge of the classics and mathematics. But botany was his first passion and most of his leisure time was spent in the field.

He became acquainted with many leading naturalists of his day including Sir James Smith of Norwich, who bought the famous collection of Carl Linneaus, and Dawson Turner, who attributed his interest in botany to Wigg's influence. He gave up the school and worked as a clerk in Turner's bank from 1801.

His favourite area of research was marine algae and he added several new species, found in the Yarmouth area, to the British list. Although Wigg's herbarium and notes have not survived, it is said that his specimens might have been incorporated within Dawson Turner's collection. Certainly, Wigg's industry is clear from the many references made to him in the works of his contemporaries. He was elected an Associate of the Linnean Society in the early 1800's. Wigg died in 1829 and is buried in the General Cemetery close by Yarmouth's market place.

Dawson Turner was born at No. 40 Middlegate Street in October 1775, the son of a banker, and was educated at North Walsham Grammar School and then privately, by the renowned Norfolk botanist, the Rev. Robert Forby, Rector of Fincham. He entered Pembroke College, Cambridge, to read divinity but stayed no longer than a year as, on the death of his father, in 1794, he returned to Yarmouth to run the family's bank.

He communicated with many leading naturalists of his day, and sent a constant supply of rare plants to James de Carle Sowerby whose "English Botany" was begun in 1790, while exchanging more locally common species with distant botanists. Turner studied seaweeds along the Norfolk coast and his researches led to his first botanical work, "A Synopsis of British Fuci" of 1802. Three years later the pioneering "Botanists guide through England and Wales" appeared. Written in collaboration with Lewis Weston Dillwyn, Turner had circulated around the country a printed four page questionnaire seeking plant records, thus providing not only a topographical handbook for collectors but also leading the way for what has become known as "network research". Turner's most celebrated work, the four-volume "Fuci..." was published between 1808 and 1819 and contained 258 plates, some of which were drawn by William Jackson Hooker, later of Kew Gardens, who became Dawson Turner's son-in-law. This mammoth undertaking was Turner's last botanical work. The remainder of his time was taken up mainly with historical research and consolidation of his huge collection of books and manuscripts. Towards the end of his life, he moved away from the Bank House in Hall Quay, down to London where he died in 1853.

The Yarmouth born brothers Charles and James Paget came from a large family. Their father Samuel, a successful brewer, had amassed a considerable library including many natural history books. Their mother was a gifted writer and painter and an avid collector of natural objects, especially seashells and corals. With parents eager to promote an interest in these things, and a circle of friends which included a number of prominent county naturalists, the brothers had every opportunity to pursue a study of natural history.

Charles specialised in insects. His initial sorties gathered some 750 species from the area and he began corresponding with many other naturalists. Meanwhile James was guided in botany by the biologist Thomas Palgrave, a nephew of Dawson Turner. Through him he was introduced to William Hooker and other leading Norfolk naturalists. He exchanged coastal plants with inland collectors and built up a nearly complete herbarium of the flora of the district. The culmination of the two brothers' efforts was the "Sketch of the Natural History of Yarmouth and its Neighbourhood" of 1834. The book is some 120 pages long and includes lists of birds, mammals, reptiles, fish, flowering and non-flowering plants and insects found within a radius of ten miles of Yarmouth. The "Sketch" was one of the first of the local faunas which became a feature of the 19th century, and remains a valuable record of the status and distribution of Norfolk wildlife of over 160 years ago. James left for London shortly after its publication and, of course, became the eminent surgeon. Charles remained in Yarmouth studying entomology. He provided all the insects listed in the "Sketch" 766 species, and to these he added a further 100. Unfortunately Charles' health was not strong. He had been an invalid from the age of 13, and the strain of the ailing brewery business contributed to his untimely death in 1844. Yarmouth had lost one of its most gifted naturalists.

Born in a typical Yarmouth row in 1857 of humble parents, Arthur Patterson triumphed against adversity to become one of Norfolk's finest naturalists. Early influences included the schoolmaster William Wallis and Benjamin Harwood, the Yarmouth shoemaker and wildfowler. Employment was a constant problem and, from an insurance agent, in about 1877 he passed through the varied professions of postman, pedlar, showman, (his specimens included a whale and an armadillo) warehouseman, zookeeper in Preston and Dublin till finally he became a full-time school attendance officer. This post gave him the settled regime needed to pursue fully his naturalist ambitions. All the time, though, he had been writing profusely; to newspapers, "The Zoologist", and for publication. "Seaside Scribblings", the first book of many, was published in 1887.

His main interests were birds and marine life, especially fishes. In 1901 he published the "Catalogue of Birds of Great Yarmouth" which was expanded to "Nature in Eastern

Norfolk" 1905. The section on fishes in the latter included many important county records of discoveries by Patterson while patrolling the wharves and beaches of his hometown. Other books and articles dealt with the wildlife of Breydon Water and the activities of the watermen who eked a living from the estuary - "Wildlife on a Norfolk Estuary" 1907 and "Wildfowlers and Poachers" 1929.

Respected beyond the bounds of his county, Patterson was elected an Associate of The Linnean Society in 1935, the year of his death.

Natural History Societies have existed in the town since 1889. The present Society, founded in 1927 included among its members the nationally renowned microscopist Harry Edward Hurrell. Born at Norwich he was at one time laboratory assistant with Caley and Corders, the manufacturing chemists; he attributed this experience to giving him a taste for microscopy. Hurrell contributed many observations of microscopic pond life to learned journals and societies. He also became an expert in the technique of making microscopic preparations and these were often exhibited at the meetings of the Quekett Club and the Royal Microscopic Society in London. While corresponding with the leading specialists in freshwater life he also actively encouraged young students and was popular at field meetings of the Great Yarmouth Naturalists' Society.

Hurrell's connection with Yarmouth was that he was manager of the Eastern Daily Press office here for 53 years, retiring in 1933. A keen musician, he was active in local orchestras and choirs. He died in 1942 and is buried in Gorleston cemetery.

One of the most remarkable of past Society members was Philip Ernest Rumbelow. A plumber by trade he was, in his spare time, a learned amateur archaeologist and naturalist. An expert on East Anglian prehistory, the Roman period, churches and old Yarmouth, he was also renowned for his knowledge of local botany, geology and microscopic life. He constructed his own microscopes, which he took on the Society's field excursions, and made cameras and lantern slides with which he illustrated his popular lectures. Unassuming and naturally retiring it was Rumbelow who guided the Great Yarmouth Naturalists' Society from its earliest days through to the 1950's. Ever present on the societies outdoor meetings, he was always on hand to give advice and resolve a dispute. Throughout his career as an inspired amateur, Philip Rumbelow maintained a record of his observations, which extended to 25 volumes of notes, letters and illustrations. He died in 1954 at his home in Rodney Road, aged 75 years.

Edward "Ted" Ellis, the man most qualified to be called the "father" of the Great Yarmouth Naturalists' Society, was born on Guernsey in 1909. At the age of eleven, his family moved back to Norfolk, to Gorleston where the young naturalist soon began exploring the cliffs and shoreline. Leaving school at the age of fifteen, Ellis worked for a time at Gurney's zoo and aviary at Keswick Hall. But in 1928 he was successful in applying for a job in the Natural History Department at Norwich Castle Museum, where he stayed until 1956. He then began a freelance career of writing and broadcasting, deriving inspiration from his idyllic home at Wheatfen, in the Yare Valley.

An internationally renowned expert in the study of microscopic fungi, Ted Ellis was nevertheless acknowledged by most as an all-round naturalist. The breadth of his knowledge was extraordinary and the inspiration he gave to young students was enormous. As a teenager he became "assistant" to Arthur Patterson and from this friendship was forged the link between the modern and golden ages of Breydon and its adjoining marshes. Ted Ellis died in 1986. A great friend of Yarmouth and Norfolk, the church at Surlingham was crowded for the funeral. Three months later, Norwich Cathedral was packed for a service of thanksgiving for his life.

Robin Harrison was a wildfowler and naturalist who became the recognised authority on Breydon Water and its marshlands. Born in 1908 he lived and worked in Yarmouth all his life. He contributed weekly articles to Eastern Evening News between 1935 and 1985, based mainly on his observations of the birdlife around Breydon. He also wrote two small books; one about Scroby Island and one about Breydon Water. A stalwart of the Great Yarmouth Naturalists' Society, Harrison was also a leading figure in the establishment and running of Breydon Water Nature Reserve.

Michael Seago was born at Brundall Gardens in 1926. He began his birdwatching on Breydon and the adjoining marshes and this inspired him to write a regular feature for the Yarmouth Mercury, which he continued from 1949 to 1986. He stayed in Norfolk, working as an actuary at Norwich Union, and became not just the county bird recorder, but the unrivalled authority on Norfolk's birdlife. His "Birds of Norfolk" appeared in 1967. From the mid 1970's he reached a wider audience when he began the "Birds of Norfolk" feature in the Eastern Daily Press, and on the death of Ted Ellis in 1986, he began contributing notes to the paper's daily countryside feature. His unassuming manner hid a deep passion for the Norfolk countryside, its landscape and wildlife. He served on many committees and was influential in the development of ornithology in the county and the advancement of the conservation movement in East Anglia. Michael Seago died in 1999, sadly just before the publication of the new "Birds of Norfolk", in which he played a major role.

Chapter 3 — Designated Places Within Our Area

Within Great Britain each country has a Conservation Agency with the power to designate areas of conservation significance; this confers on such areas a measure of protection from development. The agency for England is English Nature. These areas are usually referred to by the use of initials and this chapter will attempt to give a brief explanation as to what these stand for, how and why they are selected and what they are intended to protect.

The best known of these areas is probably the S.S.S.I. or to use the full title, Site of Special Scientific Interest. These were first notified in 1949 primarily to introduce a consultation procedure for developments that required planning permission. Significant changes were made in 1981 to include owners wishing to carry out forestry or agricultural operations in S.S.S.I's in the consultation process. These areas are selected against published guidelines and are intended to be the best examples of our wildlife habitats, geological features and land forms.

Examples of local S.S.S.I's are Breydon Water and the North Beach, both so designated for their importance to wildlife.

National Parks are extensive areas of high landscape value and are designated by the Countryside Commission. Whilst the Broads do not carry the title of National Park they have enjoyed a similar status, in conservation terms, for several years.

Environmentally Sensitive Areas (E.S.A's.) are areas of high landscape and conservation value. In exchange for management agreements, farmers in these areas may qualify for incentive payments to manage the land in a specific manner. These agreements run for ten years and the level of payment is based upon the amount of management required.

National Nature Reserves (N.N.R's.) are also designated by English Nature and are sites which are managed primarily for the purpose of nature conservation. These are areas considered to be of national or international importance to wildlife and are either owned and managed by English Nature or safeguarded by a Nature Reserve Agreement (N.R.A.) There are two such reserves in the area covered by this book, Winterton Dunes and Martham Broad.

Ramsar Sites are named after the place in which the convention was signed that agreed the designation of these areas of internationally important wetland; this is Ramsar in Iran. These sites are listed by the Secretary of State on the basis of advice given by English Nature and will already be S.S.S.I's. The convention requires the promotion, conservation, and wise use of wetlands. It also calls for new wetlands to be designated where development on existing sites becomes necessary in the urgent national interest. Breydon Water is a Ramsar Site and, as this book was being written, Halvergate Marshes was declared as a new Ramsar Site.

Local nature Reserves (L.N.R's.) are declared by a Local Planning Authority as opposed to English Nature and are managed by voluntary conservation organisations. The designation is a commitment by the Local Authority to manage the site to safeguard it from damage. The greater part of the Breydon Water S.S.S.I. is also designated as a Local Nature Reserve.

There are two further major nature conservation designations that are of interest to us and they both came about as a result of European Directives. The European Directive on the Conservation of Natural Habitats and of Wild Fauna and Flora, known as the Habitats Directive, led to the designation of Special Areas of Conservation (S.A.C's). These areas are intended by the directive to form a European network of important habitat types and habitats of important species known as Natura 2000. No development may take place that affects the integrity of such a site. The other directive, known as the Birds Directive, The European Directive on the Conservation of Wild Birds requires that the habitats of listed birds are protected. The United Kingdom designation for these areas is Special Protection Area (S.P.A). and these sites are also part of Natura 2000. Both S.P.A's and S.A.C's were already notified as S.S.S.I's. That's a lot of jargon in one sentence, hence the need for this chapter. Examples of S.P.A's in our area are again Breydon Water and the North Beach.

Within Norfolk there are many small areas, mostly in private ownership, that are very important to wildlife. In order to identify these, the Norfolk Wildlife Trust (then the Norfolk Naturalists' Trust) was commissioned in 1983 by English Nature (then The Nature Conservancy Council) and the Norfolk County Council to survey the whole county. This was undertaken with the full support of the County Land Owners' Association and the National Farmers' Union. The results found that 82% of the area surveyed was either arable, improved grassland or urban. The remaining 18% was divided into three categories of conservation importance; the best were called "C" sites and are now known as County Wildlife Sites.

There are currently more than 1,300 of these sites in Norfolk and whilst they do not have the statutory protection afforded to S.S.S.I's their value is recognised in the Norfolk Structure Plan. The wildlife interest is taken into account when dealing with planning applications that involve these sites. As the vast majority of these sites are in private ownership the designation, County Wildlife Site, confers no access rights to either the general public or nature conservation organisations; it is just a recognition of the sites conservation value.

These sites, together with S.S.S.I's, represent the minimum of natural habitat to maintain the current level of wildlife in the County. The survey work is ongoing and much work is done by the Norfolk Wildlife Trust in identifying new sites and providing advice on land management for conservation.

Part 2
The Flora and Fauna in their Setting

Chapter 1 — Woodlands

THE HABITAT

At the end of the ice-age, as the temperature began to rise and the ice to retreat, the cold damp soil would first have been colonised by hardy plants and low growing shrubs. These each helped to dry out the ground and then as they died and decayed, to build up the soil. This would slowly have created conditions in which trees could take hold and eventually thrive.

Trees with windblown seeds, such as willow and birch, would probably have been among the first, followed by pine and hazel. As conditions improved, in terms of both soil and climate, other varieties such as oak, elm and lime gained a hold each settling and developing well, in various areas of the country, until most of lowland Britain was covered by trees.

Man's influence on woodland probably began about 6,000 years ago with his need for agricultural land to raise livestock and grow crops; this influence grew, as timber became a requirement for fuel and building materials.

The ancient management techniques of coppicing and pollarding are still in use in woodland today. Coppicing is the cutting of a tree to almost ground level leaving a stump, or stool, from which new timber shoots, creating, after about 10 to 20 years a sizeable crop of timber for fuel, fencing or light building work. This technique used on a regular rotational basis provides a constant supply of such timber.

One drawback of coppicing was, that where grazing animals were present the new shoots would be eaten thus preventing the regeneration of timber from the stools. The method of harvesting which overcame this was pollarding; this cut off the bole of the tree at a level that could not be reached by grazing animals, and so preserved the harvest of new timber. Many samples of such work can be seen today at places like Bradfield Wood, a Suffolk Wildlife Trust Reserve, and at Foxley Wood owned and managed by Norfolk Wildlife Trust. Sadly neither of these woodlands are in the area covered by this book.

Man's use of woodland has very much determined its use as a wildlife habitat, the flora and fauna varying greatly with the type of woodland as will be illustrated in this chapter.

TREES

Of the 33 trees native to Britain only seven species ever formed natural woodland of any significance. They are the Pedunculate and Sessile Oaks, Alder, Ash, Beech, Pine, and Birch.

The Pedunculate or English Oak *Quercus robur*, very common locally, is a deciduous tree of hedgerows and especially old woodland. It is a rugged looking tree, its leaves and flowers

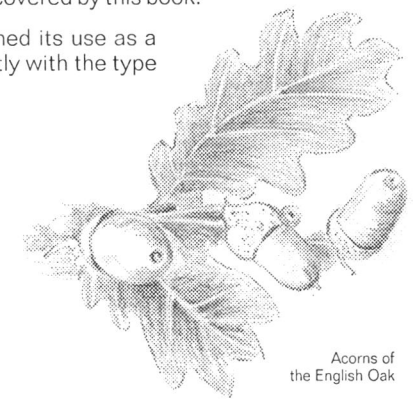

Acorns of
the English Oak

appearing together in May, the male flowers hanging in slim catkins and the female flowers from the tip of shoots. The Sessile Oak Q. *petraea*, an altogether more handsome tree is an even earlier native. It is finer and faster growing than the pedunculate with a longer and straighter bole. Sessile means without stalk and one way the trees can be identified is by looking at the acorns. Those of the Sessile Oak have no stalks and grow straight from the tree and those of the Pedunculate are attached by a stalk.

Alder *Alnus glutinosa* lines the banks of the broads and rivers in this area and has colonised most of the wet woodland, fen and marshes; the presence of Alder usually indicates a rich soil.

Another very common native deciduous tree is Ash *Fraxinus excelsior*, growing up to 25m (80ft) in oak woods, scrub and hedgerows. It is a tall, spreading tree that flowers in May-June and fruits in October-November; the leaves appear after the flowers. It is easily recognised in its winter state by its coal black buds.

The Beech *Fagus sylvatica* is another deciduous native and grows to 40m (130ft). It can live up to 200 years and thrives on well-drained soils of either chalk or sandy areas. It has a very dense canopy and whilst it will trap enough light to grow up under other trees nothing will grow under it. Tall and stately with a smooth bark it flowers in April-May and fruits in September-October. It is one of the last trees to shed its leaves often over-wintering with many still in place.

A locally common tree, especially on sandy soils, the Scots Pine *Pinus sylvestris*, is a native to Britain but in England, Wales and Ireland all the woods are planted.

Known as the "lady of the woods" the Silver Birch *Betula pendula* is also a deciduous native and grows to 25m (80ft) on light soils and heathland but it is rare on chalk. It flowers in April and fruits in July; its prolific fruiting is a great attraction for winter flocks of small seed eating birds such as siskins and redpolls It can be easily distinguished from the White Birch *B. pubescens* by the black diamond shaped fissures on its bark.

A native of South East England and dominant in some areas of Epping Forest, the Hornbeam *Carpinus betulus* is rather rare in this area; it flowers April-May and can grow to 30m (100ft). It has been planted extensively in the North of England and into Scotland mainly in parklands and gardens. Like the beech it holds its leaves well into the winter months. The timber is extremely hard and has been used for making cartwheel hubs and cog wheels for windmills.

Much planted for forestry, the European Larch *Larix decidua* is an introduced species. It is found locally in parks and woods and is commonly self-sown.

The Yew *Taxus baccata* is widely planted in churchyards and woodlands throughout the area. The Irish Yew *T. fastigiata* can be distinguished from the common Yew by its more upright growth. It is a very long lived tree with many of the big churchyard Yews being over 1,000 years old. It flowers in March-April and bears little red berries later in the year.

Rowan *Sorbus aucuparia*, also called the Mountain Ash, is quite common in this area especially on sandy soils; it is very often planted. It is a native to Britain and will grow further up hills than any other tree; up to 1,000m (3,000ft). It flowers in May and is well known for its clusters of red berries in the early autumn. In the north-west in a good autumn the leaves turn to yellow, then orange and finally to bright red but the changes are usually far less spectacular in this area.

Known by most schoolboys as the conker tree, the Horse Chestnut *Aesculus hippocastanum*, derives its name some say, from the likeness of its "conker" fruits to the sweet chestnut. Others believe that it is derived from the horseshoe shaped scar that remains when a leaf is removed. The buds are large, brown and sticky and the leaves are long stalked in six segments. When in flower the trees resemble giant candelabra with the white flowers being held upright on upward curving ends of branches. Thought by many, because of familiarity, to be a British native, it is in fact native only to a few mountains in Greece and was not introduced to Western Europe until after 1600.

Small-leaved Elm *Ulmus minor Ssp. minor* is a common tree of the area, widespread in hedgerows and has many intermediate forms.

Sweet Chestnut *Castanea sativa* with its shiny green leaves is locally quite common especially at Somerleyton and Lound. It flowers in July and produces its fruit, in very prickly cases, in good time for Christmas roasting.

One of the later native colonisers, the Crab Apple *Malus sylvestris*, can be found in woods and hedges. It flowers in May and carries small greenish apples in the autumn. Its wood is very dense and close grained and is highly regarded by wood turners as it works and polishes very well. On much common land the crab apple is less frequent than the wild orchard apples, which have grown from discarded pips of cultivated varieties. These tend to have darker pink flowers and larger fruit than the Crab Apple.

Grown in Britain for some 400 years, but originating from the Western Mediterranean, the Holm Oak *Quercus ilex* known also as the Evergreen Oak, was much valued as a shelter belt tree as it can withstand sea winds and was also planted as shade for livestock. It is the largest evergreen broad-leaved tree in the country.

The Oregon Grape *Mahonia aquifolium* is an established alien occasionally found in our area; it was originally planted as close cover for game.

PLANTS

When one thinks of woodland plants it is likely that the first that springs to mind is the Bluebell *Hyacinthoides non-scriptus*. This plant is very common locally being present in most woodland hedgerows. The flower is not always the blue normally associated with the name; some plants have pink blossom and some white. Although the removal of bluebell bulbs from the wild is illegal, recent scientific research has shown that trampling the leaves is the biggest threat to their survival.

The Common Dog Violet *Viola riviniana* is also very common within the area and can be found in most of our woodlands and wayside lanes. It has a violet-blue flower and the long stalked leaves are heart shaped, those at the base of the stem forming a rosette.

A quite nondescript plant with very small pale flowers Dog's Mercury *Mercurialis perennis* should not be handled as it is extremely poisonous. It is generally found in shady places and carpeting woodland floors.

A favourite flower, the Primrose *Primula vulgaris* is a genuine harbinger of spring. It is quite common in the woods and plantations of the area although it is becoming less so.

Dog Violets

A plant of the drier woodland, Wood Sage *Teucrium scorodonia* is also to be found on heaths and dunes. It can be recognised by its square stem and toothed and wrinkled leaves; it has a taste and smell which resembles that of hops and has been used as a substitute for it in some areas.

Enchanters's Nightshade *Circaea lutetiana* is another plant of the woods and shady places and can be found in most of the British Isles. It is occasionally found in the woods of our area including Damgate at Acle and Blocka Lane off the Beccles Road.

Great Willowherb *Epilobium hirsutum* is an erect, hairy, herbaceous perennial 80cm-150cm tall, with terminal leafy clusters of conspicuous relatively large flowers 1.5cm-2.5cm across. The popular name for Great Willowherb, "codlins and cream" is probably derived from the petals which are rosy pink at the top rather like "Codlins" or cooking apples, with creamy white underneath. This is very common in damp or wet places especially in this area and is not confined to wooded places but is very widespread.

BIRDS

Surprisingly to most people both Grey Herons and Cormorants nest high in trees and can therefore be called occasional woodland birds.

Grey Herons nest in scattered colonies in East Norfolk, particularly at Burgh Castle, Fritton, Herringfleet and around the Flegg broads. Former sites included nesting colonies at Mautby Decoy Wood and at Wickhampton; both are now long deserted.

Nearly 200 years ago Cormorants nested in immense numbers around Fritton Lake and perhaps elsewhere, but declined through shooting. With the recent increase in numbers and breeding in both Essex and Cambridgeshire, colonisation of tree-lined inland waters in this area is a distinct possibility again. Up to 300 roost in trees around Fritton Lake during the winter months and this site is perhaps the most likely area for re-colonisation.

Birds of prey are represented by breeding Sparrowhawks and to a lesser extent Kestrels, whilst Common Buzzards are scarce but regular winter visitors. A pair of Red Kites successfully bred in woodlands between Yarmouth and Lowestoft in both 1996 and 1997 to the surprise of many people. Both adults were considered to be of Scandinavian origin rather than from the recent re-introduction programme. Birds were present in the same area in 1998 and 1999.

A very common bird of woodlands is the Wood Pigeon whilst the Stock Dove is certainly present, but in much smaller numbers. The Turtle Dove is a summer visitor but has declined alarmingly since the late 1960's. Many are unfortunately shot on migration in southern Europe with French hunters being the main culprits; the purring call of the Turtle Dove in woodlands is now sadly rarely heard.

Cuckoos remain annual summer visitors in small numbers, arriving here in mid to late April and are equally seen in woodlands as in open countryside.

Our commonest woodland owl is the Tawny Owl whilst only occasional nesting Long-eared Owls are recorded. A pair of these nested successfully in the Fritton area in 1998 in secluded fir trees with others perhaps overlooked. Pairs nesting in the Winterton area have been detected by the distinctive calls of the young Long-eared Owls, likened to that of a squeaky gate. Little Owls are likely to be found in more open areas, but will occupy areas on the edge of woodlands.

Wrynecks are a former nesting species in the area; the last recorded nests being in the early 1920's in the Fritton district. Of the Woodpeckers, the commonest is the Great

Spotted Woodpecker, whilst the smaller Lesser Spotted Woodpecker has declined in numbers in recent years; most bird watchers now consider it difficult to see one in the course of a year. The larger and more colourful Green Woodpecker maintains a presence in small numbers in suitable areas. The Lound Waterworks area and the East Somerton woodlands are good sites and the spring calls of the male are very distinctive giving rise to one of its local names, the yaffle.

The Woodlark is a bird of woodland clearings and since the great gale of October 1987, which resulted in the creation of many areas of suitable habitat, this species has increased considerably in East Anglia. Prior to this, last breeding records in this area were at Belton Common in the mid 1950's, but in recent years, Woodlarks have bred at Ashby, Herringfleet and Winterton and been present at other sites in spring and summer.

Robins, our typical Christmas birds, are still widespread in local woodlands, but not so the Nightingale. There has been a widespread decline in this species in the last decade and nowhere is it common.

Mistle Thrushes are still reasonably abundant in localised areas and both Blackbird and Song Thrush can be easily found, although the latter species has decreased.

Of the warblers, Blackcap, Garden Warbler, Chiffchaff, and Willow Warbler are typical woodland species, whilst Wood Warblers are possible in summer but may be overlooked.

The tiny Goldcrest is a typical bird of conifer stands, but is also found in mixed woodland and is still reasonably common. The Firecrest is also recorded in small numbers, but it is mainly a passage migrant and an occasional winter visitor.

One of the latest spring migrants to arrive is the Spotted Flycatcher, which is a typical species of open woodland; all have departed by early October.

Long-tailed Tits are birds of woodland edges, whilst Coal Tits are exclusively found in coniferous woodlands. Both Willow and Marsh Tits are less common and more frequently seen in broadland birch and alder carrs. Great Tits, Blue Tits and Treecreepers are all reasonably abundant and the colourful Nuthatch can still be found in the more mature woodland areas.

The Golden Oriole is rare, but an occasional bird on passage will stay for a few days. These birds prefer stands of Black Poplar, which are almost unknown in this area.

The shy, but versatile, colourful Jay is better known and increasing. A bird mainly of the deciduous woodlands, it is often seen shuffling between oak trees for acorns which it will store for the winter.

Now very common in all areas the Magpie formerly only nested in wooded districts and much the same applies also to the Carrion Crow. A number of very large colonies of Rooks nests occur around the edges of woods, particularly around Haddiscoe, Reedham, Burgh Castle and Wickhampton, but these are birds of more open areas.

Of the Finches, the Chaffinch is a widespread breeding species in areas of mature trees and one of our commonest birds. The Greenfinch prefers more open areas and will nest in gardens with large trees, whilst Siskins and Lesser Redpolls are both exclusively woodland species, but scarcer.

The Crossbill is the finch of coniferous woodlands and occasionally nests in the area, the last occasion at Ormesby in 1967. It is very irregular in its visits, but between June and September are often good times to see this fascinating bird.

The Bullfinch is a bird of forest edges, plantations and orchards, but has sadly decreased in all areas though because of its shyness is often overlooked.

Very uncommon indeed is the Hawfinch; the last nesting records being for 1912. A bird of deciduous and mixed woodlands, a few recent mid-summer records suggest that a pair or two may still breed in the area. It is very shy and unobtrusive and makes itself known by its call-notes, but often goes undetected for months at a time.

MAMMALS

Hundreds of years ago wolves, wild boar and bears could be found in the woods and forests around Britain but not so today. In the wooded areas around the Yarmouth area, various mice, voles and shrews, squirrels, bats, hedgehogs and occasional deer are the usual species to be found.

Of the smaller rodents the Wood Mouse *Apodemus sylvaticus* is the more common species. It tends to forage around in the leaf litter and feed on large quantities of tree seeds that have fallen to the ground. Often referred to as the field mouse or the long-tailed field mouse, it is fairly common in the wooded areas of Lound Waterworks, Fritton Woods (sometimes referred to as Waveney Forest), Belton Common, in several of the drier wooded areas around the broads and in one or two other smaller wooded areas. During autumn as the weather starts to turn colder it may attempt to inhabit garden sheds, greenhouses or even find its way into dwellings in an attempt to escape the cold spells of weather during the winter months. It really means no harm but is nevertheless an unwelcome guest. It may also be attracted into sheds or other outhouses at other times of the year especially if grain products are stored such as wild birds food or foodstuffs for rabbits and other pets. Its main enemies are owls and birds of prey such as the Kestrel, but of course cats account for quite a large number of fatalities.

The infamous Grey Squirrel *Sciurus carolinensis* was first recorded in Norfolk in 1963 and began to spread dramatically. The first records for the Yarmouth area date from the mid 1970's. The numbers seen in Yarmouth and the surrounding districts soon increased until they were so common that no one bothered to record them any longer. It is a sad fact of life that while their most engaging ways make them attractive to people, the more destructive side of their nature tends to be overlooked. Those encouraged into private gardens may well repay their hosts by taking their young birds or their eggs, a trait for which they are well known. Visitations to private gardens seem to be quite common these days and most owners are generally tolerant of them, for there are still many people who are not aware of the amount of damage they do. They continue to inhabit most woodland in this area but there does seem to be some slight decrease in their numbers in the last two years. If this is the case then there are those that will be rejoicing in this news for they do an enormous amount of damage in the countryside. During the summer months the dreys built by Grey Squirrels go un-noticed, being hidden by the tree canopy, but when the leaves fall and the branches are once again laid bare, the dreys become obvious and the squirrels themselves are seen as they cavort among the branches. Like Jays they tend to bury acorn stocks in the leaf litter on the ground to call on when other food is in shorter supply. Occasionally small clusters of buried acorns are forgotten or not required, and small groups of oak seedlings spring up, perhaps a dozen or so from one small area.

Muntjac Deer *Muntiacus reevesi* are occasionally seen in some wooded areas. During the last four or five years they have been recorded regularly at Lound Waterworks, usually the records are of fleeting glimpses of animals that have been disturbed. From a distance the casual observer may mistake the Muntjac for a dog for they are no bigger than some medium sized dogs, and their bark is sometimes similar. Records have also come from Blocka Lane near Fritton where three were spotted together on one occasion quickly making off into denser woodland when disturbed. Occasional sightings have been made at

Belton Common and in the Waveney Forest but often the droppings are the only indication of their presence in a particular locality. The creature does appear to be expanding its range and it is inevitable that more and more sightings will be made.

Several unconfirmed reports have been received of the Chinese Water Deer *Hydropotes inermis* but members of the Great Yarmouth Naturalists' Society recorded a firm sighting at Belton Common during an evening ramble. A single specimen has been recorded at Lound Waterworks during July 1999, the first record of this species to emerge from this location. Once again their expansion will lead to more sightings.

Occasional sightings of the Red Deer *Cervus elephas* have been made around the wooded areas surrounding Fritton Lake. Three were recorded at Browston and odd sightings have been made in Blocka Lane and in the Waveney Forest though it is believed that these are wandering creatures from the Somerleyton estate. They are a magnificent sight and quite worthy of a photograph should the cameraman find himself in a satisfactory position when they appear.

Stoat *Mustela erminea* are occasionally seen in woodlands where they have been recorded climbing trees attempting to steal eggs from birds nests. They are a great enemy to the rabbit and naturally where rabbits are observed, the possibility of a stoat being seen is likely. They wreak havoc when they enter the burrows of the rabbit causing the whole population to depart the nest rather rapidly. It is in this way that the stoat accounts for most of the rabbits taken, for when in the open it is unlikely that the stoat will out-run the rabbit. The stoat is easily differentiated from the weasel by the black tip to its tail and its generally little larger size. Although Weasels *Mustela nivalis* are occasionally seen in woodlands they are not strictly a woodland species and consequently have been mentioned in more detail under Farmlands.

There have been a number of unconfirmed reports of Mink *Mustela vison* being seen in the area but Mr Bryan Witherstone of Cobholm, who runs a ferret rescue service, confirms that there are quite a number of them around and that they are in fact increasing. This opinion is supported by increased sightings reported in the Norfolk Bird and Mammal report published by the Norfolk and Norwich Naturalists' Society. A confirmed report has been received of a male specimen seen taking a dead mole at Aldeby pits on 12th June 1999. One or two reports of Mink being seen at Lound Waterworks and Belton Common have also been received but are unconfirmed. The Mink is not native to Britain but was introduced from North America during 1929 for its fur and the fur farms in existence at that time were delighted to include this in their list of products. Inevitably there were escapes and creatures attaining their freedom, began to breed in the wild. Known as feral mink they have spread throughout many areas of the British countryside including Norfolk and have found the Norfolk waterways to their liking. The first confirmed record of them in the Yarmouth area is of two being shot on the allotments to the north of Yarmouth close to the Bure in 1984, where several chickens had been killed but not eaten. This creature has a particular liking for water voles and has consequently contributed to further reducing their already declining numbers. They are similar in appearance to other members of the *Mustelidae* such as stoats and weasels but are a little larger in size. Their coat is usually very glossy, being a very dark brown and sometimes even black and the males are usually larger than females.

Bats in the Yarmouth area are not very well recorded and records are only of incidental sightings from a few members. Pipistrelles *Pipistrellus pipistrellus* are the most commonly seen and have been recorded at Lound Waterworks, Hopton, Belton Common, the Waveney Forest, Blocka Lane and in various parts of Yarmouth and Gorleston. This species is perhaps the most likely to inhabit roof spaces of domestic buildings. The Noctule Bat

Nyctalus noctula has also been recorded at Hopton and Lound Waterworks and in Damgate Lane at Acle.

It is certain that other bats may be present within the area but the lack of reliable records prohibits mention of other species.

INSECTS

1. Butterflies

The Purple Hairstreak *Quercusia quercus* is regularly seen in the higher branches of oak trees in Blocka Lane and Lound Waterworks, with odd specimens seen in Sandy Lane at Belton. Doubtless they are to be found in several other locations but records are somewhat sparse, possibly due to the fact that they tend to stay in the higher branches of the trees and are rarely seen closer to the ground. J. E. Knights a local naturalist and former member of the GYNS produced a paper in 1898 entitled "Notes on Local Butterflies" and in referring to this species he knew it only from Reedham. Those with an interest in seeking this quite attractive species would be advised to view the tops of oak trees through binoculars in different locations.

The White Admiral, *Ladoga Camilla* is a scarce species found locally at Upton Fen near South Walsham. Although the location is just outside the area of this book, mention should nevertheless be made of its appearance there, where at times it may be fairly abundant. Outside that location however, records are indeed scarce. A single specimen was recorded in Blocka Lane on 7th August 1993 being chased by Swallows and a further record was obtained from Belton Common on 4th August 1996. Due to its slow but sure expansion in Britain, this species should be carefully sought in suitable wooded locations within the recording area for it may simply be a matter of time before it is found more regularly. When netted and temporarily contained in a suitable receptacle, careful examination will show just how beautiful this creature really is. The undersides of the wings clearly out-shine the uppers with a mixture of white, black and shades of brown from a golden brown through to dark brown with the general patterning showing through to the upper-sides of the wings.

The Comma *Polygonia c-album* is rather scarce in the area, never being seen in large numbers; two or three seen together is a reasonable sighting. It is a somewhat conspicuous butterfly due to its jagged wing edges, which serve as an aid to its identification. This species lays its eggs on nettles, hop and elm leaves and with careful examination they are not too difficult to find. It has been recorded in numerous locations within the area but usually only in ones or twos. The adults hibernate through the winter and emerge in spring, being one of the early butterflies seen in spring sunshine.

A most attractive butterfly of the woodlands, though sadly not very common with us, is the Speckled Wood *Parage aegeria*. Only occasional sightings have been made at Belton Common, Lound Waterworks and Waveney Forest.

The Brimstone *Gonepteryx rhamni* is a beautiful creature, especially the male, which displays a bright sulphur-yellow upper wing. The male specimen is surely one of the easiest of British butterflies to identify. The female, which is a much paler yellow, may be mistaken while on the wing, for one of the whites but when at rest the wing shape distinguishes it from these. They are frequently encountered by many of the broads where their food plants are found. Alder Buckthorn *Frangula alnus* and Purging Buckthorn *Rhamnus cathartica* are the larval food-plants and are very scarce which no doubt accounts for the species being uncommon in the eastern and southern parts of the recording area.

Species such as Small Tortoiseshell *Aglais urticae*, Peacock *Inachis io* and Painted Lady *Cynthia cardui* are not normally regarded as woodland species. but they are occasionally seen in this habitat. Likewise all three of the white butterflies and even the Meadow Brown *Maniola jurtina* are perhaps seen passing through.

The Ringlet *Aphantopus hyperantus* has a preference for dampish areas, often those verging on woodland; the edge of Damgate marshes and Lound Waterworks both provide this requirement where it has been recorded as well as in many other similar locations. This species too may be seen venturing into the denser woodland temporarily leaving its usual haunt.

Ringlet

Within the recording area there is much scope for the butterfly enthusiast and many beautiful locations in which to find them and undertake serious study.

2. Moths

This category covers possibly hundreds of species of moths, a large number that unfortunately must be omitted from this publication since many of them are very specialised and require detailed examination in order to identify them. Those included below are well worth a mention as being typical of the species to be found in or around woodlands.

The Buff-tip Moth *Phalera bucephala* is perhaps one of the more common woodland species to be encountered. It is quite distinctive, with buff coloured tips to the wings so that when at rest they give the appearance of a twig that has been broken. The caterpillars are also quite conspicuous being yellow-orange and having longitudinal black bands. They often appear in groups and have a particular liking for oak trees, although they may also be found on sallow or hazel. This species occurs in most of the wooded locations within the area. At times hundreds of the caterpillars have been noted within the Waveney forest. The adults are found on the wing in June and July and rest on the bark of trees during the daytime.

A very striking moth is the Black Arches *Lymantria monacha* being mainly white with black zigzag markings on both wings. Found between July and September they inhabit woodlands and fly at night. Males are more active than females and the latter may often be found resting on tree trunks during the daylight hours. It may be found in most of the coniferous and deciduous woods as well as mixed woods in the area, although it is by no means common.

One of the greenish species found in woods is the Merveille-du-Jour *Dichonia aprilina*. The moth itself is quite conspicuous but when at rest among lichens on the bark of trees, it becomes extremely difficult to spot. It is usually found from August to October around oak trees and is most often found at rest on oak trunks during the day; it is present in many wooded areas where oaks are found.

The Sycamore Moth *Acronicta aceris* as its name would suggest is associated with the sycamore although it may be found on other trees. The moth itself is not very conspicuous but the caterpillar is an extremely attractive creature around 40mm long and is covered with dense tufts of long yellow and orange hairs from head to tail. There are four pairs of dark orange tufts on the back and a line of black spots, each containing a white spot, extending from head to tail. They may be found in most locations between late July and occasionally into September.

In keeping with its common name, the wings of the Pebble Hook-tip *Drepana falcataria* are turned back looking like a hook on each end. It is frequently found at Lound Waterworks and the Waveney Forest feeding on birch and alder and is also occasionally found on heathland.

The Clouded Border *Lomaspilis marginata* is found in damper woodland and is common at Lound Waterworks, Blocka Lane and many other such locations. It is a fairly common species and is fairly widespread.

The November Moth *Epirrita dilutata* as its name suggests is seen on the wing during November, though it is around from September through to December. This species could perhaps be described as somewhat drab, being of various shades of grey and when at rest on bark is easily overlooked due to its near perfect camouflage.

Another fairly common woodland species, The Engrailed Moth *Ectropis bistortata* was, during 1998 very common everywhere even away from woodland. When resting on bark they become very difficult to spot since it blends in perfectly with any lichen on the trunk. It is found in many wooded locations within the recording area.

The Bordered White Moth *Bupalus piniaria* is usually found in coniferous woodland and is a common species in the Waveney Forest between late May until sometimes late August, if the weather remains favourable. It likes to fly fairly high up among the uppermost branches, occasionally flying down to the ground but soon returning to the higher parts again. The larva feed on the needles of conifers sometimes to pest proportions.

Of the larger and more spectacular hawk-moths only one or two can really be termed as woodland species. Although several have names which associate them with trees, such as the Lime Hawk-moth *Mimas tiliae* and the Poplar Hawk-moth *Laothoe populi* these are not really woodland species.

The Pine Hawk-moth *Hyloicus pinastri* is associated with coniferous woodland and is occasionally seen in the Waveney Forest among the pines. At night it is busy but during the day it tends to rest on the trunks of pines and is very well camouflaged. In the experience of the author it has almost always been found at rest in pairs. The only records that have come to light are from the Waveney Forest but it is extremely likely that they are to be found in other locations where conifers are present.

The Broad-bordered Bee Hawk-moth, *Hemaris fuciformis* is not strictly a woodland species but it inhabits woodland clearings such as Belton Common where it has been regularly recorded. In this location, when disturbed, it has been noted that it nearly always resorts to the more densely wooded areas and in this respect may be considered to be associated with woodland.

3. Other Insects

Woodland insects are numerous enough to be able to fill the pages of a reasonably sized book in their own right. In a volume such as this, it is impossible to afford anything but a mention of just a few of the more common, or indeed rare, insects that are to be found in this habitat. There are microscopic insects that dwell in the leaf litter, there are species that live only in the canopy of trees and there are yet others that spend most of their lives deep in the fissures of the bark of trees. These may all deny the non-specialist recorder the opportunity of adding them to their notebooks. Many others are nocturnal and consequently are only seen by torchlight.

There are indeed many insects that require catching in order to identify them but these have generally been avoided in favour of those that may be easily identified by the amateur using standard reference books on insects.

The Common Earwig, *Forficula auricularia* is by far the commonest of the earwigs and is often found under loose bark in woodlands. The female is an excellent mother, she lays her eggs and will nurture them, turning them regularly and licking them clean. In the humid atmosphere under bark the eggs would otherwise quickly become affected with mould. They are to be found in most wooded locations throughout the area and are extremely common.

The Green Lacewing *Chrysopa perla* has a liking for deciduous woods and is fairly common between May and August. It is quite an attractive creature and is to be found throughout the area.

Several of the shield bugs are woodland species, or are at least associated with woodlands. The Hawthorn Shield Bug *Acanthosoma haemorrhoidale* as its name would suggest is associated with hawthorns but is not restricted to woods, it is also to be found in open habitats where hawthorns grow.

The Forest Bug *Pentatoma rufipes* is found in woodland areas as well as more open habitats on a wide range of trees and shrubs. It is a common species and found in most areas.

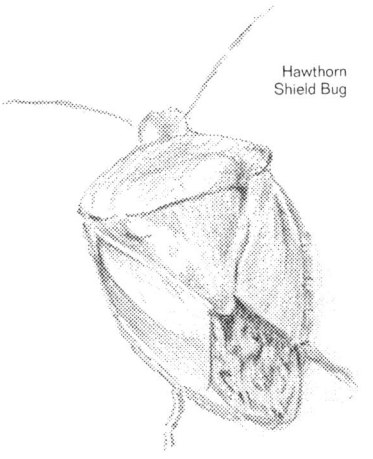

Hawthorn Shield Bug

The Parent Bug *Elasmucha grisea* is an interesting species. After the female has laid her eggs they are closely guarded by both parents and are often to be seen on birch leaves during spring and early summer. Like tiny pearls the eggs are protected until they hatch and the nymphs are then protected in a similar fashion by the parents until they are able to fend for themselves. Many other insects lay their eggs and leave them and after hatching the youngsters are left to their own devices. At times the nymphs accompanied by the parents are to be seen marching along branches or twigs as they search for food. They are commonly found in most locations where there is birch.

The tiny little Common Flower Bug *Anthocoris nemorum* spends most of its time in the leaf litter and is quite difficult to find for it is indeed very small. It is also to be found on a variety of flowers and plants. It feeds on aphids and red spider mites and is thus useful in the garden. It is extremely common in most locations.

Aphids are to be found aplenty in woods sucking the sap from the leaves of woodland trees, though thankfully there are many ladybirds and hoverfly larva to help keep their numbers to within tolerable proportions. A small dark coloured aphid with no common name but known to science as *Adelges abietis* is found on spruce. This creature deserves mention for its ability to cause pineapple galls to grow among the needles on the tree which mature between June and July, producing a new generation of aphids that will attack other spruces and conifers. Records received would suggest that they are not very common but should be found in locations where spruce is growing.

With regard to beetles there are many to be found in woods. Several of the larger *Carabidae* or commonly called ground beetles are to be found here. Most of the members of this family are identified by the markings on the elytra or wing cases and much enjoyment can be gained in trying to sort them out. There are numerous smaller beetles that require much closer examination to be able to identify them.

The Violet Ground Beetle *Carabus violaceus* is perhaps the more commonly encountered of the *Carabidae* and is easily identified because of the bright violet sheen to the edges of its elytra. They are nocturnal creatures and hunt for slugs and other prey and by day they lay up under stones or logs or may even be found in the soft tissues of rotting stumps. This species may also be found in gardens and other habitats. It is a common species and has been recorded at Waveney Forest, Lound Waterworks and many other wooded areas.

If the dead body of some animal should lay on the ground, it will not be long before the burying and rove beetles make an appearance. They are not strictly woodland creatures but will readily appear wherever there is carrion to be found. Some of them will dig tunnels underneath the dead creature and gradually drag the corpse down into the excavation until it is completely buried. The females then lay their eggs around the corpse in order that the emerging larva can feed on the rotting flesh. The rove beetles will also feed on the flesh though they do not resort to burying.

The Devil's Coach-horse or Cock-tail *Staphylinus olens* is probably familiar to most people for although it is often found in woods it occurs variety of other habitats including gardens. When disturbed it raises its scorpion-like tail and opens its front jaws but this is really a show for it is harmless to humans. During the day it hides under stones or other debris and comes out at night to hunt slugs and many kinds of invertebrates. It is a common creature and found everywhere.

Several species of ladybirds are found in woods, some associated with coniferous trees and others found almost everywhere. Species like the common Seven-spot Ladybird *Coccinella 7-punctata* is abundant but is not specifically a woodland species.

The Eyed Ladybird *Anatis ocellata* is usually found on, or at least in close proximity to, coniferous trees. It is one of the larger species to be found and is quite an attractive creature. There is quite a lot of variation in its markings just to make things interesting for the observer.

As its name would suggest the Pine Ladybird *Exochomus 4-pustulatus* is found among pines. It is almost black with red spots and does not appear to be very common in the area, in fact the only records that have been received are from Belton Common. It is worth searching among the branches of pines for this ladybird, for it surely must appear in other locations where there are pines.

There are several weevils to be found among the trees in our woods. One such is the little Birch Leaf-roller *Deporaus betulae* which rolls up part of a leaf into a cigar-shaped container and lays a single egg inside, the rolled up leaf providing both protection and food for the hatching larva. This species also uses Hazel and Alder leaves for this purpose. Each leaf-rolling weevil has its own peculiarities with respect to the shape and construction of the leaf-roll and with a little research they are easily identifiable. The larvae of some weevils are leaf miners, that is to say they move around between the upper and lower epidermis of the leaf itself. This provides food and protection. Others may prove to be pests when they are found among stored grains.

Many parasitic wasps are to be found here, some parasitising the caterpillars of butterflies and moths while others attack the larvae of various beetles. Generally called Ichneumons they appear in all sizes large and small. The largest Ichneumon to be found in this area is *Rhyssa persuasoria* and it is a truly fearsome looking creature. This species has been recorded at Lound Waterworks, Belton Common, Waveney Forest, Damgate wood at Acle and at various other locations. There are several other specimens that behave in much the same way that are occasionally to be seen in woods though not really to be considered as true woodland species. These creatures are useful in that they help to keep the numbers of certain other insects down that might otherwise become pests.

REPTILES AND AMPHIBIANS

Woodland or wooded areas are found in various locations, some adjoining heathland such as at Belton Common, some are close by water or damp areas such as around several of the broads and consequently there may be some overlapping of species. For example frogs and toads are not generally considered to be woodland creatures but where the woods extend to damp areas it is not uncommon to find them at times, when they are on the move. The same may be said of our two common snakes.

The Adder *Vipera berus* is more often to be found in heathland environments, whereas the Grass Snake *Natrix natrix* prefers damper conditions but both species are to be found in quite densely wooded areas at Belton where the differing habitats join each other.

The Common Lizard *Lacerta vivipara* is found at both Belton Common and Waveney Forest in the slightly more damp conditions; they are often chanced upon in woods if one casually wanders through.

FUNGI

There are in excess of 3,000 species of the larger fungi to be found in Britain although only a fraction of these are to be found in Norfolk. There are certain species that are only found where coniferous trees grow, some only grow among broad leaved trees and some are less selective and may be found growing with either.

Of the species to be found only among coniferous trees is the *Suillus luteus*, commonly known as Slippery Jack, which is found during autumn mainly around Scots pines, and present in the Hopton House Estate, Lound Waterworks and Waveney Forest and probably several other wooded areas where there are pines. The False Chanterelle *Hygrophoropsis aurantiaca* is also commonly found among conifers during autumn as is the bright red and attractive species known as the Sickener *Russula emetica* which is quite common throughout the area. The Rufous Milk-cap *Lactarius rufa* is another associated with pines. Almost all of the milk-caps are peculiar in that they exude a latex milk from the gills when handled or broken; the latex is often whitish but varies somewhat depending on the species.

Amanita phalloides, known as the Death Cap, is a highly poisonous species and may be found growing under oaks and should be avoided at all costs. It is the most poisonous species known to man and contains many toxins. Most species of the group *Amanita* are poisonous.

The smell of the Common Stinkhorn, *Phallus impudicus* may well be apparent before it is seen. The smell causes flies to be attracted to the slimy cap that assists in the spread of the spores; it is found frequently and is usually associated with dead wood buried below the soil. This species may also occasionally be found growing in gardens.

Like the previously mentioned Sickener which is associated with pines, there is an equally attractive, similar looking species called the Beech-wood Sickener *Russula mairei* that is associated with beech trees. Many other types of Russula are also to be found.

The Common Yellow Russula *R. ochroleuca* for example, is a common species and is easily identified.

Various Puffballs grow in most areas among the leaf litter and require some close examination in order to identify them. Most notable is the Common Earth-ball *Scleroderma citrinum* which may grow up to 100mm across the cap; they tend to have a preference for sandy soils in woods.

There are also many so-called bracket fungi to be found; these usually grow out from the trunks of various trees with some being quite distinctive. The Beef-Steak Fungus *Fistulina hepatica* and the Artist's Fungus *Ganoderma applanatum* are notable, though perhaps the most common is the Birch Polypore *Piptoporus betulinus* which only grows on the trunks of birch trees. It attacks only sickly or aged trees gaining access through wounds or where branches have broken off; it is invariably fatal to the tree.

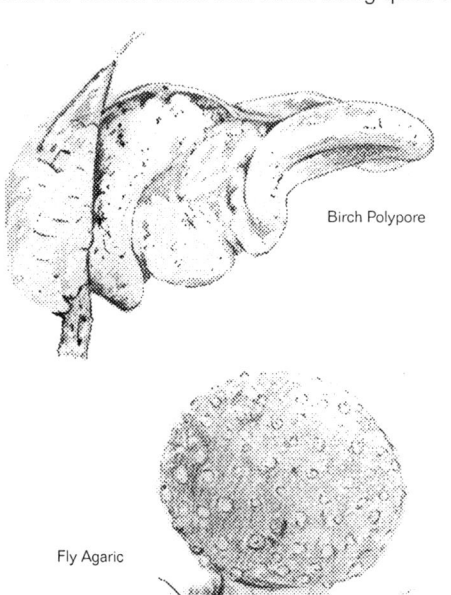

Birch Polypore

The Wood Mushroom *Agaricus silvicola* grows in both coniferous and deciduous woods among the leaf litter whereas the smaller species Sulphur Tuft *Hypholoma fasciculare* grows only on the stumps of both types of tree.

Most books dealing with fungi state that the Fly Agaric *Amanita muscaria* is to be found growing under birch and a few state that it may also be found occasionally growing under conifers. In the Waveney forest and at Lound Waterworks, it may, at times, be found growing under both.

Fly Agaric

There are hundreds of other species to be found growing in the woodlands within the area, far too numerous to be mentioned individually within the scope of this publication.

Chapter 2 — Marshland

THE HABITAT

Marsh, or lowland wetland, can be described as ground that does not dry out. Although it does not necessarily hold standing water the ground is always waterlogged. The original marsh in our area is divided into two main categories, either coastal grazing marsh or fen.

Coastal grazing marshes, which can in fact spread far inland, vary in salinity from salt marsh on the coast to freshwater marsh inland. The origin of these marshes goes back to Roman times when areas of coast were enclosed by sea walls to prevent tidal flooding, a task more or less completed by the Victorians. With tidal flooding prevented, the salt marsh vegetation begins to give way to plants of fresh water grassland. Much of this inland marsh has, over the years, been drained with greater and greater efficiency in order that it can be used for agricultural purposes. This is evident when one travels the Acle Straight passing fields of cereal crops where once there was marshland. Berney and Halvergate marshes, due to positive management for wildlife, retain high water levels and in fact are flooded at certain times of the year.

The development of the inland marsh will depend upon the nature of the soil, either acidic and poor in minerals or slightly alkaline and rich in dissolved nutrients. In the first case a permanent marsh may develop into a bog, normally associated with poorly drained upland areas, and where the soil is nutrient rich the most likely development is to fen.

Fenland develops from permanent marsh that is rich in nutrients and has a slightly alkaline soil. The predominant plant is likely to be the Great Fen-sedge *Cladium mariscus*, which is much valued for its use in thatching. The frequency of the harvest of this sedge will play an important role in the fen development. Where there is little or no harvesting the fen will tend to dry out and be invaded by woody plants such as Bittersweet *Solanum dulcamara*. Willow scrub and Alder will follow until eventually the fen may dry out completely becoming an oak wood. Commonly a four-year rotational harvest is used and this maintains the sedge as the dominant species. Where a more frequent cutting regime is practised, other species such as Wild Angelica *Angelica sylvestris*, Yellow Loosestrife *Lysimachia vulgaris* and Hemp Agrimony *Eupatorium cannabinum* will gain a foothold creating a rich and colourful habitat of immense wildlife value.

PLANTS

If one looks at the area covered by this book, the map will show that about 80% is covered by marshland, either arable or grazing. The flora of this area is varied with substantial populations.

The commonest plants to be found on the drainage marshes are grasses. The dense flowering heads of Cock's-foot *Dactylis glomerata* are said to look a bit like the foot of a cockerel, hence its name. It is also a very common sight on roadside verges and waste ground. The majority of British grasses are difficult to identify when not in flower, but Cocksfoot is an exception.

Another common grass is Yorkshire-Fog *Holcus lanatus*, a loosely tufted and pale coloured grass often seen in dense swathes in this habitat. Other grasses often found here are Common Bent *Agrostis capillaris*, Marsh Foxtail *Alopecurus geniculatus*, Meadow Foxtail *A. pratensis*, Rye Grass *Lolium perenne* and Annual Meadow-grass *Poa annua*; this latter mentioned grass can be found in all habitats.

Common Reed *Phragmites australis* is undoubtedly the most conspicuous plant of the marshland area as it is the largest native grass of the British Isles; Burgh Castle Lagoon is one of the biggest reedbeds in our area. Reed Sweet-grass *Glyceria maxima* is another large common grass of the dykes and waterways.

Sedges are perennials and many can be found in the wet and damp situations of marshland while others are of dry habitats. Some of the more common Sedges that can be found on the marshes in our area are Common Sedge *Carex nigra*, Greater Pond Sedge *C.riparia*, Lesser Pond Sedge *C. acutiformis*, Tufted Sedge *C. elata* and False Fox Sedge *C. otrubae*. The Divided Sedge *C. divisa* is rather rare but can be seen on the Berney Marshes Reserve.

The network of dykes that criss-cross the marshes is the ideal home for Common Duckweed *Lemna minor*, the most frequently found of the duckweed species. Also likely to be present are Fat Duckweed *L. gibba*, Ivy-leaved Duckweed *L. trisulca* and Least Duckweed *L.minuta*; these have all been recorded in the dykes.

Often mistaken for the excellent salad plant, Watercress *Nasturtium officinale*, the similar looking Fool's Watercress *Apium nodiflorum* is also very common in the dykes. Its name is a reference to those who would mistakenly collect it only to find that it is totally unpalatable.

Water Fern *Azolla filculoides* which is a native of North America has established itself well in this area and is frequently found in dykes and ponds.

Potamogetons *Potamogeton Agg* require specialist knowledge to identify and so are mentioned only as a grouped species; they are very common in the dyke systems.

Occasional records of Arrowhead *Sagitaria sagittaria* have been noted in the dykes, the single sexed flowers appearing from May to September.

The White Water Lily *Nymphaea Alba* is a native to Great Britain and is found in unpolluted ponds and fens. The white flowers are unmistakable and the leaves smaller and rounder than those of the yellow water lily. The Yellow Water Lily *Nuphar lutea* or Brandy-bottle as it is known locally is again a native.

Marsh Marigold *Caltha palustris* is a perennial forming large tufts and is found in many ponds and rivers. Once widespread this species appears to be on the decline but it is still found on marshes and by pond sides and in wet woods.

Although Water Crowfoots *Ranunculus sp* are fairly frequent in Norfolk, the occurrence in our recording area is very small. All have white flowers with a yellow base to the petal and grow in water and on mud. One place in which they may be found is the Filby Bridge Nature Reserve.

Water Dock *Rumex hydrolapathum*, with its large lance-shaped leaves, which can be up to 1m long, is a frequent, and easily recognised, plant of the dykes.

Although its name suggests otherwise the Water Violet *Hottonia palustris*, is not a violet at all but is a member of the Primrose family; many of the dykes by the Weavers Way have large stands of this.

Branched and Unbranched Bur-reed *Sparganium erectum* and *S. emersum*, Water Plantain *Alisma plantago aquatica* and Bogbean *Menyanthes trifoliata* as well as the unmistakable Bulrush *Typha latifolia* (once known as Reed Mace) can be found around many dykes and waterways. Yellow Flag *Iris pseudacorus* is extensive and very common in the area. Brooklime *Veronica beccabunga* is related to the Speedwells and is very common in dykes and on watersides. Marsh Pennywort *Hydrocotyle vulgaris* is a plant that is well established in and out of the water and its leaves can cover large areas of land.

Both Marsh Bedstraw *Galium palustre* and Lady's Bedstraw *G. verum* are common on the marshes in our area: Fen Bedstraw *G. uliginosum* is less so.

Marsh Thistle *Cirsium palustre* is frequent in the area including Lound and Breydon Water and Marsh Sow Thistle *Sonchus palustris* which became quite rare early in the 20th Century is now commonly found.

Common Fleabane *Puticaria dysenterica* as its name implies is quite common and widespread in wet places as is Common Valerian *Valeriana officinalis*.

Although very rare in the area, Nodding Bur Marigold *Bidens cernua* can be found growing in the dyke by Tesco's on Caister Road.

Recorded frequently by rivers and wet places are the Willows. Crack Willow *Salix fragilis*, which is very common on riverbanks, plays an important role in preventing soil erosion by holding the soil together with its long roots. Some other Willows found in the same habitat are White Willow *Salix alba* and Cricket Bat Willow *Salix alba var.caerulea*.

Turning our attention to the salt marsh, a small area around Breydon, we find the Sea Milkwort *Glaux maritima*, a plant with creeping rooting stems and stalkless fleshy leaves in pairs; the stalkless flowers are borne singly at the junction of leaf and stem during June-August.

The next chapter deals with estuaries and other saltmarsh plants will be dealt with in this context.

BIRDS

Prior to drainage, these wet marshlands were home to large populations of nesting and wintering wildfowl and waders, including Lapwing, Black-tailed Godwits, Ruff and Redshank. Baskets upon baskets of their eggs were regularly sent to the London markets in the spring by the marshmen and in the winter, wildfowl in large containers were sent to the same destinations. Avocets nested on the lower Bure levels by the Stracey Arms until about 1805, whilst Black Terns were reported in huge numbers nesting on the Upton marshes in 1818. By 1845, following enclosure awards and drainage, all had departed. Spoonbills formerly nested in trees at Reedham in the early half of the 17th century, but at what date they ceased to nest is unknown.

The introduction of steam drainage on these marshes in the 1840's, and the building of both the Acle New Road and the railway line between Yarmouth and Acle at this time, all brought considerable change to the Halvergate Marshes. Water levels dropped and these powerful steam pumps were almost able to cope with the heaviest of rainfalls. The progression of drainage continued with the introduction of diesel and then electric pumps in the late 1930's. The last drainage windmill ceased work in 1953 and, at present, all these marshland levels are well drained and mainly dry for most of the year. The exception, however, is the Berney reserve at the extreme western end of Breydon Water owned by the RSPB and this is well flooded, especially in winter.

Birdlife, despite drainage, is still of great interest on these marshlands and many species are to be found. Grey Herons, although decreased in numbers since the 1950's are still reasonably common and it would be unusual to travel by train or by road between Yarmouth and Acle or Reedham

Grey Heron

without seeing one. Grey Herons formerly nested in large numbers in trees at Mautby, Reedham and Wickhampton, but these heronries are now deserted. At present, Burgh Castle holds a small, but increasing, heronry with others at Fritton and elsewhere. The creation of the RSPB Berney Marshes Reserve in 1986 has created additional feeding areas and it is not unusual to see up to six Grey Herons here together.

Cormorants are recent users of the larger dykes in the marshes and there is no doubt that their numbers have increased. It would appear that most of them are of the continental race of Cormorant *sinensis* rather than that of the British race *carbo*, which is more marine in its habits. Many of the Cormorants roost in considerable numbers at Fritton Woods and are a regular sight as they fly to and from the marshes each morning and evening.

Little Grebes frequent the larger dyke systems in summer and then move into the rivers and broads in winter. The loud trilling call of the male is frequently heard in spring and early summer.

Little Egrets are recent, almost annual, visitors in spring and at other times, following increases on the continent, notably north-western France. As many as four have been seen together.

Mute Swans are a real feature of these marshlands and dyke systems and pairs breed on most levels. In winter, birds congregate in herds on flooded levels, particularly at Berney, and feed on winter wheat and oilseed rape, as well as grass. It is not unusual to see up to a hundred together but smaller herds are more frequent.

In winter, Bewick's Swans from Siberia arrive, usually in late October and frequent areas of wetter marshes and also arable marshes. Peak numbers appear in January and February and up to 700 have been recorded.

MAMMALS

In many cases the Mole *Talpa europaea* is the most common mammal that inhabits the marsh and evidence of this is borne out by the numbers of molehills to be seen. It finds the softer slightly damp soil of the marsh easier to dig through and as a consequence some of the molehills may be so large as to half fill a wheelbarrow. On occasions a Heron may be seen standing by a molehill waiting for the occupant to make an appearance and the large bill will be thrust into the loose soil to grab the unsuspecting mole. When caught in this way moles scream pitifully but usually to no avail.

Another mammal inhabitant of the marsh is the Brown Hare *Lepus capensis* and although nowhere near as common today as in the past is still often encountered. The Berney marshes between Breydon Water and the Acle New Road is one of the foremost locations in Britain for this species with up to 45 being seen together. Elsewhere they are less common and two or three seen together is a reasonable sighting.

The Rabbit *Oryctolagus cuniculus*, although sometimes seen on the marsh does in fact prefer the drier areas where it can dig its burrows without fear of them collapsing.

Foxes *Vulpes vulpes* are probably at least as common on the marshes today as in the past. They hunt young water birds for food and are not bothered if it is a young duck or gosling but they may not always eat them entirely.

Stoats and weasels are occasionally seen hunting mice and voles and such like. A stoat in ermine has been seen along the banks of Breydon Water.

The Bank Vole *Clethrionomys glareolus* like the Water Shrew *Neomys fodiens* is by no means as common today, in fact there is some concern regarding their survival in the area. Although they are both occasionally to be seen they are indeed quite rare within our recording area.

Of course in the past, the Coypu *Myocaster coypus* would have found a worthy spot within our recording system but today they are extinct in Norfolk. An extensive trapping programme carried out during the seventies and eighties saw to that; nevertheless they do find a spot in the natural history of our county.

We look forward to the day when the Otter *Lutra lutra* is once again to be seen on and around our marshes as it once used to be. They are being bred in captivity and then released into the wild and the signs are very good for the future. A great deal of monitoring is on-going at present to determine whether they are increasing or are still in danger of disappearing. They were once a familiar creature of our waterways although their liking for fish caused much concern to the angling fraternity, especially if they had stocked a section of river with expensive fish, but then it has to be remembered they are only doing what comes naturally. Time will tell if the releasing programme has been successful or not but it has to be said that the return of the otter to our waters would make a welcome addition to the fauna of our area.

INSECTS

1. Butterflies

Perhaps the most splendid butterfly of all that is likely to be encountered is the magnificent Swallowtail *Papilio machaon*. Its range is now largely restricted to the Broads of Norfolk and parts of Suffolk where the food-plant of its caterpillar, Milk Parsley *Peucedanum palustre* is to be found growing in quantities large enough to support the species. Generally its appearance is usually restricted to the broads area but occasional sightings are made at other locations within the area.

The Brimstone *Gonepteryx rhamni* may occasionally be seen in marshy areas. The male is a beautiful sulphur yellow colour and requires little knowledge in order to identify it. The female is much paler and when seen on the wing could possibly be mistaken for one of the whites. This is probably the earliest of the butterflies to be seen in spring; Brimstones hibernate through the winter and it is usually the males that are seen first.

The Small Tortoiseshell *Aglais urticae* is probably the most commonly found butterfly. It makes its appearance early in spring straight from hibernation and is found almost everywhere where there are good clumps of nettles. A great deal of fluctuation occurs in its numbers, in some years it is by far the most numerous butterfly to be seen whereas in other years it may even be scarce.

The Peacock *Inachis io*, though perhaps slightly less common than the small tortoiseshell, is often seen in good numbers. It also has a liking for stinging nettles on which its eggs are laid, and is fairly common throughout the area.

The Painted Lady *Cynthia cardui* is a species that lays its eggs on various thistles that are found growing on marshes. Numbers may fluctuate greatly with some years being known as Painted Lady years. One such year was 1996 when they were seen probably in their thousands. In other years merely the odd few specimens may be recorded. When seen in the numbers of 1996 they provide a spectacle that lingers within the memory for a long time to come. During 1996 they were seen right across the marshes throughout the area. Thistle heads often bore several resting specimens on the same plant, in fact hardly a plant could be found that did not carry at least one of these beautiful creatures. Their eggs too, could be found very easily while they were around in such numbers.

The Orange Tip *Anthocharis cardamines* lays its eggs mostly on the Cuckooflower *Cardamine pratensis*, a true marsh plant and Garlic Mustard *Alliaria petiolata*. The male of this species displays the orange tips to the wings, hence its name, while the females may be mistaken on the wing for specimens of the white butterflies. Careful examination of the plants mentioned may reveal the tiny bright orange egg, a single egg to each plant as the caterpillars tend to be cannibalistic and if two caterpillars were to hatch on the same plant one would eat the other. Such are the wonderful and often mysterious ways of Mother Nature.

Occasionally the Red Admiral *Vanessa Atlanta* may be seen around stinging nettles though never in large numbers. This species like the Painted Lady is a migrant to Britain from North Africa arriving here in numbers varying from year to year.

The Comma *Polygonia c-album* on the other hand, is a hibernating species taking up winter residence in such as sheds, out-buildings and roof spaces and emerging during early spring. It too has a liking for stinging nettles and though not generally a marshland species it tends to inhabit any area where the caterpillar food plants are to be found, the food-plants being nettles, hop, sallows and occasionally elm.

Other butterflies such as the Meadow Brown *Maniola jurtina* and the Gatekeeper *Pyronia tithonus* may also be seen at times on the marshes passing through, but they are not considered to be true marshland inhabitants.

2. Moths

Several species of the so-called China-mark Moths *Nymphula spp* are found in the marshes. They are unique among British moths in that they lay their eggs in water on the undersides of floating leaves. The caterpillar constructs a cocoon for itself from pieces of the leaf and attaches it to a plant stem and pupates inside. When the time comes for emergence, any time between June and August, the moth leaves the water and begins a nocturnal lifestyle. If a net is swept through vegetation close by the water one or two adult moths may be disturbed during the daytime when they are at rest.

Where the Common Ragwort *Senecio jacobaea* is found growing then the brightly coloured Cinnabar Moth *Tyria jacobaea* may also be found. It is an extremely attractive little moth with blackish forewings with a long red stripe to the leading edge of the wing and two red spots on the outer margin. Although it is really nocturnal it is often seen during daylight hours. An inspection of the food-plant, usually Common Ragwort, may well reveal dozens of its very brightly coloured caterpillars. They are alternatively banded with yellow and black and as the result of their feeding, may decimate a plant fairly quickly. Both the moth and the caterpillar are highly poisonous and consequently birds and other predatorial creatures decline to take them. Common Ragwort is a highly poisonous plant and the caterpillars ingest the poison while feeding and although they come to no harm themselves, they would pass on the poison to any would-be predator.

The White Wave Moth *Cabera pusaria* is often found at rest on sallows and birches, it is quite a pretty moth and fairly common throughout the area.

The Latticed Heath *Semiothosa clathrata* is an extremely attractive day-flying moth that feeds on marsh clovers. It tends to have the appearance of a small butterfly of the skipper family rather than a moth.

The Blackneck Moth *Lygephila pastinum* has greyish wings with a black v-shaped mark on each. It feeds on Tufted Vetch *Vicia cracca* and although not common is seen occasionally on marshes.

3. Dragonflies

Dragonflies are commonly found in or around marsh dykes which provide excellent conditions for breeding. Eggs are laid in the water, sometimes on plant stems or sometimes merely dropped into the water so the resultant larva can find a secluded spot amidst the many plant stems until it has grown enough to be able to fend for itself. The larva of all the species is highly predatorial and captures its prey by stalking it and then leaping out to catch it by means of an appendage fitted neatly under the face, which it thrusts out at almost lightning speed. The quarry is then brought to its mouth for devouring. Anyone who has kept these creatures in the confines of an aquarium and studied their movements will appreciate just how interesting the process is.

Dragonflies *Odonata* are divided into two groups, the larger dragonflies *Anisoptera* and the damselflies *Zygoptera*. Usually the earliest of the dragonflies is the Hairy Hawker *Brachytron pratense* while the earliest of the damselflies is normally the Large Red Damselfly *Pyrrhosoma nymphula*. The Hairy Hawker can be recognised while at rest by the abundance of brownish hairs on the thorax while the Large Red Damselfly is bright red with the female having yellow bands. Identification of this species is quite simple as no other is similar at least within south-east Norfolk; it is quite common throughout the area.

The Southern Hawker *Aeshna cyanea*, the Brown Hawker *Aeshna grandis* and the Emperor Dragonfly *Anax imperator* are among the larger species to be seen and are all reasonably common given favourable weather conditions. Dragonflies dislike wet and windy conditions and on such days may be hardly seen at all. The Migrant Hawker *Aeshna mixta* makes its appearance a little later in the season than most of the other species and once again may be seen in good numbers. It is present throughout the area.

The above species of dragonflies are generally termed as hawkers, for it is their habit to fly around "hawking" ever on the look-out for a tasty morsel in the form of smaller insects which they can catch with their remarkable speed and agility in the air.

Another group known as chasers usually set their sights on their prey and will chase it until they catch it. These include the Four-spotted Chaser *Libellula quadrimaculata*, the Broad-bodied Chaser *L.depressa*, the Black-tailed Skimmer *Orthetrum cancellatum* and the Scarce Chaser *L. fulva*. The first three species of the above chasers are all relatively common whereas the Scarce Chaser is only to be found, within the area recorded, on certain marshes along the Waveney. They have been recorded on the marshes at Fritton but are generally a very localised species.

There is another group to be found here known as the darters. Generally only two members of this group will be encountered but migrant species have at times been recorded although they do not have resident status and consequently do not enjoy a place on the local list. The Common Darter *Sympetrum striolatum* as its name might suggest is the more common of the two species. At times it may be seen in its hundreds while at other times it may be quite elusive. The Ruddy Darter *S.sanguineum*, although not as common as the previous species may still be seen in quite large numbers on occasions. The species often appear in company with one another, which often helps to distinguish between them. The male Ruddy Darter is indeed a beautiful creature with the body being almost crimson red.

Of the smaller dragonflies the Large Red Damselfly is usually the first to make its appearance in spring but is one of the earliest to disappear, usually by mid-July; most of the blue species may be seen throughout the summer season.

The Azure Damselfly *Coenagrion puella*, the Common Blue *Enallagma cyathigerum* and the Blue-tail *Ischnura elegans* are all commonly seen here but the Variable Damselfly *Coenagrion pulchellum* is far less common and is very localised. With the exception of the Blue-tailed Damselfly, these blue species require a closer look in order to identify them properly. The females sometimes vary within the species, which makes them similar to the females of other species and a careful examination is therefore always required. However, with experience it may be possible to identify them with some certainty but the task is still not simple for the markings may vary from female to female of the same species.

The Red-eyed Damselfly *Erythromma najas* seems to be increasing its range slightly, though it is still not common; it may be found where there is floating vegetation such as water lilies and Frogbit *Hydrocharis morsus-ranae*. The males spend much of their time resting on the leaves of these plants while the females are more likely to be found on bank-side vegetation. This species is quite conspicuous, especially the male, for as its name suggests it has bright red eyes. It has been found in good numbers at Lound Waterworks, although numbers fluctuate from year to year.

The Emerald Damselfly *Lestes sponsa* is not often seen in large numbers, with perhaps ten specimens seen at one time being considered a reasonable sighting; it can however be seen throughout the area.

The Banded Agrion *Calopteryx splendens* is a beautiful creature with the males looking more like butterflies than damselflies when seen on the wing. It has a preference for running water but on occasions has been recorded on the marshes surrounding the Waveney and at Lound Waterworks. A single sighting has been made in the centre of Gorleston, a most unusual location in which to find a specimen such as this, but nevertheless a reliable record.

4. Other Insects

The insect life, as one would suspect, is complex and varied. There are insects that spend all of their lives in water and some that spend only part of their lives within this element. Dragonflies, as previously mentioned, Caddis flies and Mayflies for example, all spend their larval stages in water but emerge as flying adults. These creatures are all quite commonly found here. Most of the water insects are in fact able to fly and when a pond or other area of water dries up they are able to move on to find new areas of water to colonise.

A beetle such as the Great Diving Beetle *Dytiscus marginalis* spends a lot of its time in the water but when the need arises, it is well adapted to take to flight. It is quite a large beetle and is usually seen when it rises up to the surface to take in a fresh supply of air. It is highly predatorial in both the larval stage and as an adult, taking such as tadpoles, small fish and other crustaceans that dwell in the water.

The Reed Beetle *Donacia aquatica* burrows into the stems of aquatic plants to lay its eggs and the tiny larva, when they hatch, live in the stems. During summer it is to be seen on various reeds and sedges growing along the dykes and is sometimes seen in good numbers. It is quite common, if somewhat localised.

On marshes where cattle are grazed the Dor Beetle *Geotrupes stercorarius* may be found burrowing in cow dung. It is a fairly large and rounded black beetle and it spends its time excavating tunnels, with a small chamber at the end, beneath the dung. It then rolls up little balls of dung which it drags through the tunnel and places in the chamber where it lays its eggs in, or around, these dung balls; on hatching, the young larva feed on the dung. Most of this goes on underground and is not usually visible but occasionally the beetles are seen on the ground especially around dung heaps. This creature is sometimes known as the "lousy watchman", a name it has acquired due to the fact that most specimens taken are infested to a smaller or greater degree with tiny brownish-red mites. When examined under a hand lens, the mites are to be seen moving around on the creature.

It is quite a common sight during late spring and summer, when peering into a dyke or pond to see lots of insects moving around on the surface of the water. One such creature, commonly known as the Whirlygig Beetle *Gyrinus natator*, may be quite obvious. It is usually seen in groups swimming around on the surface of the water, looking like so many tiny speed boats going this way and that, producing ever increasing circles on the surface. It has peculiar eyes adapted to seeing along the surface of the water and below the surface at the same time, the eyes being divided into two sections. If alarmed, it can dive immediately, a skill that it also applies when prey is spotted below the surface. This beetle is extremely common and may be seen in groups of several dozens at a time.

Another insect that may be found moving around on the surface is the Pond-skater *Gerris lacustris*, a bug with a very apt name for it does appear to be literally skating on the surface. It has long legs with specially adapted pads on its feet to allow it to move on the surface without actually penetrating it. It moves around on the surface film, ever on the lookout for any hapless insect that may be injured or has simply fallen onto the water and cannot lift itself off. The pond-skater then attacks it and makes a meal from it. If it fails to do so then there are other surface dwelling creatures that are ready to do likewise.

The Alder Fly *Sialis lutaria* is a smallish brown fly not unlike a Caddis Fly in appearance. It has heavily veined wings and when it is at rest they are usually folded over the back forming a roof-like cover; it may be very common during the summer months around areas of water. It lays its eggs in batches on the leaves of reeds and when examined under a hand lens they look like rows of miniature brown cigars standing upright from the leaf. When they hatch, the tiny larvae usually fall from the leaf into the water below where at first they seek shelter from predators but as they grow they in turn become quite ferocious predators. The larvae spend up to two years in the water, feeding on prey slightly smaller than themselves. When they are fully grown and ready to leave the water, they find a suitable spot in the bank-side and construct small oval mud cells where they pupate for around three weeks. When they finally emerge as flying insects they are unable to feed, the sole function of the female in life being to mate, lay eggs and then die. They are quite common around the area in suitable locations.

Craneflies or Daddy-long-legs as they are sometimes called are common on the marsh. The species most commonly met with is *Tipula oleracea* but occasionally the larger species *T. maxima* is found. *T. maxima* has a particular liking for damp habitats whereas *T. oleracea* may be found almost anywhere. At times *T. oleracea* is to be seen literally hundreds at a time especially when one walks through long grass or other plants and disturbs them. Gardeners and farmers have a particular disliking for them for they produce the larva known as leatherjackets; they are notorious for the damage they cause to both arable crops and garden produce.

Where there are beds of stinging nettles found growing then certain ladybirds might well be found. The commonest of them all is the Seven-spot Ladybird *Coccinella 7-punctata* which may at times occur in large numbers. The females lay their eggs on stinging nettles and the resulting larva feed on the plants and often appear to be more numerous than the ladybirds themselves. Most people are of course familiar with the Seven-spot Ladybird from their childhood days. Locally they were known as "bishy barnabees" and there are several rhymes about them. Generally they are a fairly common beetle, found almost everywhere in reasonable numbers, but in certain years there are population explosions when their numbers increase enormously; 1959 and 1976 were such years. These population explosions are little understood and research can only really take place as and when they occur. During such explosions it would be reasonable to suppose that much more breeding and mating takes place and consequently more beetles would over-winter and numbers would be even larger the following year. This however, does not happen. Within two seasons numbers are usually back to normal and will stay that way until another explosion takes place.

The Two-spot Ladybird *Adalia bipunctata* is also often found on nettles but it is never as numerous as the Seven-spot: it is recognised by the two black spots on the elytra. There are however, varieties within the species where the elytra are black with two red spots, but they are not as common as the normal ones.

Another ladybird known as the Water Ladybird *Anisosticta 19-punctata* is only occasionally found among the Reeds *Phragmites australis* and Bulrush *Typha latifolia*. It is not at all common but where it is found there may well be several of them in the vicinity.

There is a longhorn beetle that is commonly seen in damper areas and goes by the grandiose name of *Agapanthea vilosoviridescens*. It is a magnificent beetle with huge antennae and it may seem somewhat daunting at first glance but it is quite harmless. It normally lays its eggs in stems of Marsh Thistles although other plants are occasionally used. *Strangalia maculata* is another such beetle found in this habitat and its striking black and yellow colouring can often be seen on Hemp Agrimony *Eupatorium cannabinum*.

There are of course many other insects that may occasionally be found on the various marshes within the area. They are far too numerous to mention within a small publication such as this, but armed with a modestly priced field guide such as the Collins 'Insects of Britain and Northern Europe' the insect hunter should derive a great deal of pleasure in seeking out the various insects mentioned here.

FISHES

The marsh dykes play host to several species of freshwater fish and the study of these sometimes elusive creatures, is a most interesting pastime, although the list of species is not a long one. Where pollution is prevalent the list of species is indeed confined to those that can withstand adverse conditions. The same applies during periods of extremely high tides when the water in many of the dykes may become too saline for certain species. Where they can escape the salinity they tend to seek safety but where they are trapped in the dykes, many may perish under such conditions. Roach *Rutilus rutilus* and Common Bream *Abramis brama* are two species that are more able to withstand a higher degree of pollution but even they have their limits. The little Three-spined Stickleback *Gasterosteus aculeatus* also seems able live in poor water conditions. This species used to be locally known as the "stannickle" but the name is seldom heard these days.

The dreaded Pike *Esox lucius* is common in marsh dykes and makes its living by taking fish and other small aquatic creatures. As the pike grows so does the size of its prey. When very young they will feed on such as *Daphnia* and other small copepods and as it grows it takes small fish fry and then larger and so on. On occasions it may take small ducklings and other water birds. It is a ferocious predator and spends long periods lying very still amongst submerged vegetation in wait for some likely meal to present itself. When the moment arrives, a turn of speed that leaves merely a cloud of silt behind tells the observer that it has in all probability, secured a meal. The likelihood of escape from those powerful jaws is virtually non-existent for the teeth are backward pointing preventing the hapless victim from moving forward and the cavernous mouth of a large pike would easily hold a two pound bream. Many of the larger pike may be found in quite shallow dykes during April and May for they tend to seek shallower water in which to spawn. It is not uncommon to see quite a lot of activity at the end of a shallow dyke as a hen pike makes quite a big thing of spawning. The male needs to follow the female at such times for the spawn requires to be fertilised within 40-60 seconds. Most dykes usually hold a good head of young jacks all plying their trade, causing nuisance among the other fish species.

The Tench *Tinca tinca* is not a particular inhabitant of marsh dykes but they are found occasionally. They usually prefer ponds and lakes or sometimes slow moving waters. In the marsh dykes they never grow to the sizes that they achieve in ponds and lakes, staying rather small and weighing probably no more than three quarters of a pound, a pound fish being quite a respectable specimen.

These days fishing the marsh dykes is far less practised than say twenty to thirty years ago, for there are now far superior venues that hold large numbers of good weighty specimens whereas the fish in the dykes never attain the size that their pond and lake cousins achieve. In the past youngsters fished the dykes even for the sticklebacks and a largish specimen was considered something of an achievement. Most of them served part of their angling apprenticeships fishing in marsh dykes. Small Common Carp *Cyprinus carpio*, Rudd *Scardinius erythrophthalmus* and Perch *Perca fluviatilis* are other fish species that may be found in marshland waters depending on the quality of the water and marginal vegetation. Run-off of agricultural chemicals may have a drastic affect on the dykes and dyke dwellers, whereas clean and unpolluted waters will support a greater variety of not only fish but other species of wildlife.

REPTILES AND AMPHIBIANS

If the list of fishes was a short one the list of reptiles is shorter still. The Common Lizard *Lacerta vivipara* is often found in the dryer parts of the marsh. They may occasionally be seen basking in the warm sunshine.

The two species of snakes that are found in Britain are both found on marshes. The Grass Snake *Natrix natrix* is more commonly found than the Adder *Vipera beris*. The Adder prefers dryer sandy areas rather than the damper conditions of the marsh but its liking for frogs will tempt it to this habitat. The Grass Snake on the other hand relishes the damp conditions and will often take to the water if disturbed or when pursuing prey for they are adept swimmers. It too has a strong liking for frogs and will at times take small fishes. On warm sunny mornings both species may be unexpectedly encountered as they warm themselves in the sunshine.

Toads, frogs and newts which bred here so profusely in past years, are by no means so plentiful today. It is indeed sad that recent surveys of the dyke system that have been so productive in the past, have revealed very few of these creatures. In all probability water pollution that has increased in modern times is the cause, at least in part, of their disappearance. Several diseases have run rife among the frogs in recent years and much has yet to be learned about the diseases themselves and how to combat them; a great deal of research is still in progress for the problem is not confined to Britain alone. Frogs have disappeared globally and it is causing world-wide alarm among herpetologists. However, all is not doom and gloom, for locally, the diseases have not been too prevalent so far as our records tell us which may be accounted for by the fact that frogs, toads and newts are now abundantly found in garden ponds of private houses. In this kind of habitat they are afforded a greater degree of protection from predators and the pollution usually encountered in more wild environments. To some extent this phenomenon has become something of a novelty with certain pond owners boasting to others of a greater number of tadpoles or frogs in their ponds and a small amount of rivalry has occurred. Despite this much safer outlook for these vulnerable creatures there are still some dangers, for some owners who have an over abundance of either frog-spawn or indeed tadpoles, are removing them to other waterways or private ponds thus increasing the dangers of spreading any disease that may periodically appear. Sadly, it would be much safer to destroy any surplus spawn or tadpoles.

Chapter 3 — Estuary

THE HABITAT

Breydon Water is an area of stark beauty, of endless skies and wonderful sunsets: a unique and special habitat that changes not only with the seasons but also with the tides. An inhospitable and bleak area in any but the best of weather, wide open to the elements but with a wild beauty of its own.

Although not strictly an estuary, Breydon is an inland estuarine habitat at the confluence of the rivers Waveney, Yare and Bure. This is where salt water meets fresh water and where, during the still water between tides, mud and silt carried downstream by the rivers is deposited to form vast mudflats and banks.

Breydon Water lies to the west of the town and is aligned roughly south-west to north-east and connected to the North Sea by the River Yare. It is all that remains of a vast estuary which in Roman times spread from Caister to Burgh Castle, the latter village being still situated at the south-west end. Breydon is approximately 5 kilometres long and up to a kilometre wide with a navigable channel at low water of about 100 metres wide. It is somewhat artificially constrained by the North and South walls which are now essential in order to protect the lower lying parts of Yarmouth. Just how essential was amply demonstrated by the devastating floods of 1953 when the south wall was breached.

Within the confines of the walls are the North and South Flats, which at low tide are large areas of exposed estuarine mud beloved of wading birds. There are also smaller areas of salt marsh that have built up to such a level as to be covered only by the highest of tides.

This then is the habitat in which the flora and fauna described in this chapter both survive and thrive.

PLANTS

A dominant plant on the flats of this habitat (ronds) is the Sea Lavender *Limoneum vulgare* whose pale lilac flowers make such a beautiful sight from the Yarmouth by-pass in July and August. Sea Purslane *Halimione portulacoides* is another plant that prefers the upper parts of the salt-marsh, although it will tolerate flooding, and forms mounds of silvery leaves; it bears clusters of tiny flowers in July to September.

An annual plant of the tide-line Saltwort *Salsola kali* may also be found occasionally on arable land. Another annual species of the estuary is Purple Glasswort *Salicornia ramosissima* which occurs on the ronds for as far as the saline water extends.

A close relative of the sugar beet is also found on the salt-marsh. This is the Sea Beet *Beta vulgaris ssp. maritima* which is an annual species with dark glossy green leaves and fleshy stems. Several cultivated species of Michaelmas-daisy commonly hybridise and escape and become established in the wild; one such plant bears the name Confused Michaelmas-daisy *Aster novi-belgii*.

Common Scurvygrass *Cochlearia officinalis* is a very common plant around our coast, estuaries, and salt marshes of the area but rarely grows inland. The plant is hairless, with long-stalked fleshy leaves that are heart or kidney-shaped, the lower ones forming a loose rosette; the small white flowers bloom in May or August.

A small, herbaceous perennial of the salt marshes in this area is the Sea Milkwort *Glaux maritima*. It has adapted to life in these areas where most plants cannot survive because the salt concentration prevents their roots from absorbing water. The Sea Milkwort solves the problem by storing water in its fleshy leaves. A good place to look for this is at Burgh Castle.

BIRDS

Breydon Water holds internationally important populations of wading birds and wildfowl. This area is the only representative of this habitat embraced by this book. It is a vital migration stopover locality for thousands of birds and is the most easterly estuary in the British Isles.

The deeper western areas towards the Berney Arms are favoured by Great Crested Grebes and Cormorants and in winter, by small numbers of Little Grebes. Occasionally, one or other of the three rarer grebes can be present, usually in winter when harsh weather conditions prevail on the continent.

Red-throated Divers are rare here, but at least one is seen annually. The Grey Heron is a feature at all times of the year and can often be seen standing in shallow water on the tide-line fishing in groups. In recent years, numbers have increased, largely due to protection given to the adjacent Burgh Castle nesting site. In August 1999 no less than 42 were seen in one group, a quite remarkable gathering. Little Egrets from southern Europe are a recent feature of the estuary being seen almost annually, with 4 in September 1999, the largest group seen together.

Breydon has long been famed for its extensive list of rare birds including several visits by Black Storks, White Storks and a succession of Glossy Ibis's, the last sighting of which was in the autumn of 1935. Spoonbills, locally known as 'Banjo-bills' due to their spatulate bills, have long been a special feature here. At the turn of the century, parties of up to 17 were seen. Since then however, numbers have decreased considerably, but it is still seen annually in small parties of up to 6 birds together. Most occur in the period April to August but wintering birds are not unknown.

Mute Swans are resident in varying numbers, with the slightly smaller Bewick's Swan from the high arctic, a winter visitor appearing between November and March. A few Whooper Swans, slightly larger in size than Bewick's Swan have been noted in recent winters, these birds originating from Iceland.

Of the grey geese, the Greylag Goose is increasing in numbers and it is not unusual to see up to 100 birds at the western end of the estuary close to Burgh Castle. These feral birds first nested here in 1976 after a successful introduction scheme in the late 1960's. In the same area, Canada Geese are also obvious and often associate with the Greylag Geese. Whilst Barnacle Geese are scarce, the Brent Goose is a more regular visitor in small numbers, these increasing in harsh weather conditions or when strong easterly winds persist in late autumn. The introduced Egyptian Goose is an occasional visitor and has bred, but the most obvious bird of the mudflats is the colourful Shelduck. This attractive and fully protected species is present throughout the year. Although a decrease in numbers has been apparent since the mid 1980's, several hundred seen together is not unusual. A few pairs breed, with at least 10 broods noted in 1999, the first of these usually appearing in late May or the first week of June. Virtually all adults depart in late summer to moulting grounds in northern Germany and return in stages from late September onwards.

The Wigeon is often present in huge flocks and has greatly increased in numbers; there were no less than 11,200 estimated in February 1999. All feed on the adjacent marshes, but resort to the estuary to rest and preen. Up to the 1970's Wigeon regularly fed on Eel Grass *Zostera marina* which grew in profusion on the flats, but has since disappeared, possibly due to pollution. Both the attractive Pintail and Mallard can be present in gatherings of several hundred, both feeding largely on the open mud-flats whilst smaller numbers of Teal, Shoveler and Gadwall use the site as a resting area.

Of the diving ducks, Pochard and Tufted are the more obvious, whilst in winter both Scaup and Goldeneye can be seen. During cold and severe winter spells in January and February,

Smew and Goosander are usually looked for whilst the Red-breasted Merganser can arrive at any time of the year. The occasional sea-loving Common Scoter appears whilst both Eider and Velvet Scoter have been recorded.

Among birds of prey, Ospreys seen fishing are real highlights and at least one puts in an almost annual appearance. August and September are perhaps the best months for the Osprey with the added possibility of them being seen in the Spring. Various other raptors are often seen passing over and apart from Kestrels and Sparrowhawks, the most regular bird is the Marsh Harrier. During the summer months, Hobbies are occasionally observed and in the winter, the small and versatile Merlin regularly haunts the saltings at the Yarmouth end of the estuary, chasing small waders particularly Dunlin. Its larger cousin, the Peregrine, appears annually attracted by larger prey, notably Golden Plover, Lapwing or Redshank. The best time to look for Peregrines is between late October and March and often at first light when hunting begins.

However, Breydon Water is the place for wading birds and it is on record that more rare waders records have been obtained here than at any other locality in the British Isles. Several firsts for the county were recorded here including Pectoral Sandpiper and Broad-billed Sandpiper.

The distinctive and noisy Oystercatcher is difficult not to see, and is often present in large groups. Numbers in recent years have decreased after increasing for many years. The reasons for the recent decrease are uncertain, but it mirrors decreases elsewhere in the county particularly those on the Wash. Black-winged Stilts are rare, although one stayed several days in May a few years ago.

Avocet numbers have increased tremendously, especially since 1993 and they now even nest on adjacent marshland levels. It is not unusual to see gatherings of several hundred Avocets together at high tide at the Yarmouth end of the estuary; 381 in August 1999 being the current maximum count. It is at present, surprisingly, a more common bird here than the Oystercatcher and it even winters in reasonable numbers.

Breydon is the premier site in the county for the now very scarce Kentish Plover but the almost annual sightings prior to the late 1980's are unfortunately a thing of the past. Occasional Little Ringed Plovers are seen, but it is really not a wader of the open mud-flats despite the first county records of two being recorded here in June 1943. Ringed Plovers are common throughout the year, especially in spring and autumn when birds of the slightly smaller arctic race pass through. Winter birds consist of British bred individuals that depart in March and return in October.

The Golden Plover is another wader that has increased in numbers in recent years and it is not unusual to see 7,000 birds resting together on the higher mudflats close to Yarmouth. Numbers often increase in late summer and peak in December and January; an estimated 10,300 in January 1999 remains the highest total to date. Most Golden Plovers depart by early April. The numbers of Grey Plovers are considerably lower, with birds present each month, those seen in May being in full black attire. Peak numbers occur in early October with the arrival of juvenile birds. Mirroring the Golden Plover increase, the Lapwing can appear on the mud-flats in huge congregations, with upwards of 30,000 birds in one small area. Peak estimates of 43,000 birds have been recorded and the highest numbers are seen between November and early January.

Small wading birds include the Knot, which is a passage migrant and winter visitor in small and varying numbers, and the smaller Sanderling which is mainly a winter visitor. The tiny Little Stint, a really long-distance migrant, appears in the autumn in small numbers, although a few have been recorded in late May; the similar Temminck's Stint is very rare.

(1) James Paget

NATURE IN EAST NORFOLK

(2) Arthur Patterson and a young Ted Ellis

(3) H. E. Hurrell at Microscope

(4) P. E. Rumblelow

NATURE IN EAST NORFOLK

(5) Typical Woodland Habitat

(6) Spotted Flycatcher

(7) Grey Squirrel

(8) Primrose

(9) Coppiced Hazel

(10) Scots Pine

NATURE IN EAST NORFOLK

(11) Longhorn Beetle *Strangalia maculata*

(12) Stinkhorn Fungus

(13) Sparrowhawk with prey

(14) Brimstone on Thistle

(15) Artichoke Gall

(16) Marble Gall on Oak

(17) Knopper Gall on Oak

(18) Nail Gall on Large-leaved Lime

(19) White Admiral

(20) Hawthorn Berries

NATURE IN EAST NORFOLK

(21) Typical Marshland Habitat

(22) Grey Heron

NATURE IN EAST NORFOLK

(23) Sea Milkwort

(24) Spider *Tetragantha extensa*

(25) Swallowtail Butterfly

NATURE IN EAST NORFOLK

(26) Norfolk Hawker

(27) Grass Snake

(28) Marsh Marigold

(29) Hairy Hawker

NATURE IN EAST NORFOLK

(30) Sunset on Breydon Water

(31) Avocet

(32) Common Scurvy Grass

(33) A view of Breydon from the Air

(34) Berney Windpump

NATURE IN EAST NORFOLK

(35) Typical Town Habitat - Yarmouth Cemetery

(36) Typical Town Habitat - From St. Nicholas Church Tower

(37) Song Thrush

(38) Red Fox

The White-rumped Sandpiper and the Pectoral Sandpiper are North American waders; surprisingly they have been seen on a number of occasions. A party of four White-rumped Sandpipers graced the estuary for approximately one week in the autumn of 1996, causing considerable excitement in bird watching circles all over the country. The Curlew Sandpiper is an eagerly looked for species in spring and autumn amongst the Dunlin hordes, red birds being seen in spring and early autumn with peachy coloured juveniles in late August and September. The Dunlin is by far the commonest small wader, present throughout the year and often in flocks of several thousand. Peak numbers are seen in mid-winter with passage birds in spring and autumn consisting of birds of several races. The rare Broad-billed Sandpiper has been recorded on over 20 occasions on Breydon, more than at any other locality in the country. The first British record was obtained here as long ago as May 1836. It is one of the most eagerly sought after wading birds on Breydon, but it is several years since one has been seen.

Ruff are often present but much prefer feeding on the adjacent marshland which is also the case with Snipe. Jack Snipe and the larger Woodcock are unusual here. The Black-tailed Godwit is yet another species that has benefited from increased protection and is now present in large numbers. Peak totals occur in late summer and early autumn and on occasions more than 1,000 have been carefully counted. Winter totals are smaller with a distinct spring passage often evident in March. Most, if not all, of these birds originate from the Icelandic breeding population. The Bar-tailed Godwit, in stark contrast to the latter species, has decreased somewhat, although small numbers still arrive in early May, its traditional time. However, it does now winter here and occasionally up to 60 have been noted. Whimbrels are passage birds in April and May returning in July and August with numbers appearing to be stable. It is distinctly unusual to see them after mid-September. The Curlew is a large wader whose numbers have also increased and it is present throughout the year, occasionally up to 800 and even 1,000 being counted. Noisy Redshanks nest on the saltings and are obvious birds on the flats in scattered small groups. Overall, numbers of this species have increased especially in winter, thanks perhaps, to the succession of milder winters. Both Greenshanks and Spotted Redshanks are passage birds, the latter having a tendency to winter in very small numbers in recent years, being one of the first waders back in autumn. Often these appear as early as the second week in June. The very rare Greater Yellowlegs caused considerable local excitement both in September 1975 and May 1995 when single birds stayed several days: they remain the only county records to date. A wading bird that frequents the flintstones along the estuary wall is the Common Sandpiper, another spring and autumn bird which occasionally winters. Noisy and excited groups of them can be noted in spring prior to departure in the late evening.

Phalaropes are wading birds that habitually swim, and both the Grey Phalarope and the Red-necked Phalarope are rare in our area; both have been recorded at Breydon.

Gulls of many kinds use the estuary to feed and roost. Black-headed Gulls are by far the most common while smaller numbers of Common Gulls are in evidence. Increasing numbers of the once rare Mediterranean Gull are being detected, especially at roost times. Larger gulls, the Greater Black-back and Lesser Black-back, together with Herring Gulls

Black-headed Gull

roost on the estuary in varying numbers. Strong offshore winds will considerably increase numbers roosting whilst decreases are noted in periods of little wind when birds tend to roost on the sea. Glaucous and Iceland Gull sightings are unusual and the only other large gull is the Yellow-legged Gull, a Herring Gull look-alike with yellow legs and a darker mantle. These birds breed in Southern Europe and a few are detected annually, especially in late summer. Little Gulls are passage migrants and vary in small numbers with occasional birds being recorded in winter. The high arctic Sabine's Gull was recorded in October 1881 after strong winds and constituted the first Norfolk record. Slightly larger are Kittiwakes, marine gulls that occur on the estuary only after strong onshore winds; several are noted almost annually.

The tern breeding platforms specially constructed at the north east corner of the estuary, are home to Common Terns with up to 180 pairs successfully breeding. Ringed birds have been recovered in at least ten African countries in winter. Larger than the Common Tern, the Sandwich Tern is also obvious in summer, but does not breed here. Large numbers congregate on the saltings at the Yarmouth end of the estuary in late summer. Fishing parties of the delightful Little Tern are a summer feature and it is interesting to note that two pairs bred here in 1973 rearing one chick. The large and conspicuous red-billed Caspian Tern is rare, but Breydon is now the best place to see this species in the country. Between late May and early August is the favoured time for an appearance. Both Arctic and Roseate Terns have occurred, the latter is almost annual in late summer and is perhaps the most graceful of all the terns. Of the marsh terns, Black Terns on passage in May are eagerly looked for, especially after prevailing easterly winds, with a few appearing in autumn. Rarer marsh terns include recent single visits from the White-winged Black Tern and the Whiskered Tern as well as Gull-billed Tern.

Of the small passerines frequenting the saltings, the Skylark and Meadow Pipit are the most obvious, whilst Rock Pipits are very noticeable between late September and early April. Flocks of Snow Buntings frequent the estuary walls in winter and both Lapland Buntings and Shorelarks can occur. Finches include Linnets and Goldfinches, but wintering parties of Twite are now unusual and perhaps a thing of the past.

MAMMALS

Mammals are not numerous here although Foxes *Vulpes vulpes* are seen along the Breydon walls at times, as they prowl for food; occasionally rats may be seen plying the same trade as the fox. Many years ago the local council operated a refuse tip along the south side of Breydon Water and was in operation for many years. Of course all kinds of refuse was deposited there and attracted all kinds of wildlife, mainly scavengers. Some of the largest rats seen by the author were observed here and they could be seen working their way in and out of the rubbish hoping to discover anything of an edible nature. Sometimes they were so busily engaged in turning over this and that in their quest, that one could approach them quite closely before they became aware of the intrusion. If the observer stood still for several minutes possibly as many as a score may have been in view at one time; if ever a creature dwelt amongst pure filth it must surely be the rat. Flies of all kinds hung over the rubbish especially if something of a meaty nature was dumped and their eggs would be quickly deposited and hence even more flies would appear. The old dumping site was covered with topsoil and allowed to settle for many years; it now serves as a playing field and open space amenity along the south wall.

There are a few sightings of Common Seals that venture up through the river. These have been seen close by the Berney Mill and on occasion even further upriver; Grey Seals have also been recorded.

INSECTS

Although dragonflies are occasionally seen along both the north and south walls they should not to be considered estuarine creatures, but more as passing opportunistic hunters. Similarly butterflies of various species may also be encountered often sipping at the nectar provided by the various plants found along the walkways surrounding the estuary.

FISH

The fish that may be found here are mostly salt-water species although a few specimens of pike have infrequently been seen, and indeed taken, from the saline water. Flounders *Platichthys flesus*, Smelts *Osmerus eperlanus* and Common Eels *Anguilla vulgaris* are the most common with occasional whitings and codlings that may have ventured further upriver than they probably would have wished. There is not very much fishing carried out on Breydon today, when compared with the past, but occasionally a lone angler may be seen sitting close by the new bridge with his rod and chancing his line to luck.

Chapter 4 — Towns and Villages

THE HABITAT

Man's impact on the environment is never more obvious than in our towns and villages. The continuing spread of built up areas where once there was open countryside is obvious to us all. We have all noticed ourselves saying "I remember when this was open fields" or "in my young days you could see right across to Burgh Castle from here". The change is not all bad however, we all have to live somewhere, and in this more environmentally enlightened time planners and developers have a greater awareness of the wider issues.

In this so-called urban jungle, our gardens have become oases for wildlife. They contain hedgerows, trees and shrubs, flowering plants, ponds and a whole host of other features that benefit wildlife. Indeed many of us now design our gardens to be attractive to wildlife thereby creating mini-habitats so important to the survival of many species.

There are other important "nature reserves" within towns including cemeteries, parks, and in our area at least two golf courses and a racecourse. Being on the East Coast and with some of these areas very near the sea, they often provide a first refuge for many immigrants from Europe and further afield.

There are of course many creatures that have adapted very well to town and village life. Many buildings provide sites for birds to nest, indeed the Black Redstart of our logo is well known for nesting in industrial areas. As you read on in this chapter, you will I am sure, be fascinated by the amount of wildlife that thrives as our close neighbours, or visits us from time to time.

PLANTS

Due to less maintenance than in the past, many of our streets and open spaces have become home to a variety of plants. In botanical terms many of them are classed as alien species often being garden escapes. One such plant is Canadian Fleabane *Conyza canadensis*. This wayside plant is now well established in the area and around Yarmouth and Gorleston there is hardly a crack in the pavement with a little soil available where C. Fleabane will not grow. This plant was unknown in Britain until about 200 years ago but since then it has become firmly established all over Southern England; this is a hairy annual growing up to 1.5m with a multi flowered inflorescence with small white blooms.

Annual Mercury *Mercurialis annua* is another established alien that is locally abundant and often found as a garden weed. It dies at the end of the year after seeding profusely and once the seeds are in the soil it will grow annually for many years. It shows a preference for rich soils, especially gardens, and is a native of North Africa.

Yellow Corydalis *Pseudofumaria lutea* is a well-established garden escape that can be found on walls and roadsides locally. It is an erect or spreading perennial from Europe which has pale green divided leaves and yellow spurred flowers. The seeds, which are a glossy black with an oily surface, are edible. They are attractive to ants, which may be seen carrying them off to their nests.

Both Common Ragwort *Senecio jacobaea* and Oxford Ragwort *S. squalidus* can be found in the same habitat and are both plentiful on roadside verges and waysides. Oxford Ragwort is an escape from the Oxford Botanic Gardens, first recorded in the wild in 1794.

Another established garden escape is Feverfew *Tanacetum parthenium*. This species was introduced for its value as a medicinal plant and would otherwise probably not have come to Britain. It can be seen growing in pavement cracks by walls and also in rough ground, public parks and churchyards.

Pineapple Weed *Matricaria matricarioides* was introduced into this country from North America in 1871. Conditions have suited this plant well, it has spread all around the country and become an increasingly abundant annual weed of wayside and waste places and loves being trodden under foot on paths and gateways.

Many native species also have also found their way onto our roadsides and into waste places, car parks, open spaces and even our gardens. An example of such species is the Smooth Sowthistle *Sonchus oleraceus*. It is often abundant on waste places and also cultivated land and very common on roadside verges and in public parks and churchyards. Pellitory-of-the-wall *Parietaria judaica* is a perennial herb of old walls and belongs to the same family as the stinging nettles but it lacks the sting. It is commonly found especially in and around the churchyards of the Yarmouth area where it can be very common. In the summer months the flowers of the Ox-eye Daisy *Leucanthemum vulgare* will transform the motorways and by-pass embankments into a blaze of white and gold colour. It has been planted extensively on newly constructed roadsides and is also very common in churchyards and on waste ground. There is no garden or patch of cultivated ground in the area that cannot be seen without the inevitable Groundsel *Senecio vulgaris*; its name comes from the Anglo-Saxon word "grondeswyle" meaning ground glutton. Ivy-leaved Toadflax *Cymbalaria muralis* grows on both old and new walls around the area; it is a hairless sprawling plant with glossy, ivy shaped alternate leaves scattered along the stems. Stinking Iris *Iris foetidissima* is often found growing in our local parks and churchyards and is sometimes used to brighten shady corners during the winter months with its bright red berries, the description of "stinking" refers to the smell emitted when the leaves are crushed and bruised.

Another plant very much at home in the town is the Broad-leaved Willowherb *Epilobium montanum*. The drooping buds straighten up as soon as the flower starts to open and is immediately recognised by its deeply notched petals. All willowherbs derive their common name from the slender stem and the narrow leaves which resemble those of the willow tree. It grows throughout the British Isles and is becoming very common in the towns and villages in this area especially in gardens and along the footpath edge and garden walls.

A rarity for this area, which has recently been recorded, is a single plant of the Pyramidal Orchid *Acamptis pyramidalis* found in the Yarmouth Cemetery this year (2000). It is sometimes difficult to understand how a single plant such as this can appear. It is most likely to be the result of bird activity. Another such rarity, normally a perennial to be found in old meadows and pastures, is the Green-winged Orchid *Orchis morio* which was again found in the cemetery this year.

London Plane *Platanus acerifolia* is a tree that dominates the London streets and is the most widely planted tree in many towns, including Yarmouth and Gorleston, especially in streets and parks; it can be recognized by its white patches of flaking bark. Grey Poplar *Populus canescens* and White Poplar *P.alba* are both common street trees of the area and can be seen on roadsides and in parks. The Grey Poplar is thought to be a natural hybrid between the Aspen and the White Poplar. The Horse Chestnut *Aesculus hippocastanum* is also a favoured tree in parks and by roadsides; they seldom self-seed in this habitat and nearly all are planted.

BIRDS

This habitat embraces private gardens, roadsides, parks, churchyards and cemeteries. These varied habitats hold a surprisingly large population of birds of many varieties. As with other particular habitats, birds of prey are well represented by both the Kestrel and Sparrowhawk. Both are relatively common, especially the Kestrel which nests in Yarmouth itself at several sites. These include the Racecourse complex at North Denes and on Nelson's Monument at South Denes. In 1999 it was estimated that at least five pairs were breeding in Yarmouth alone, some of those feeding their young on Little Tern chicks from the colony on the North beach.

One or two pairs of Red-legged Partridges have bred at Yarmouth South Denes for several years and odd birds have appeared occasionally elsewhere, even in gardens. Pheasants are common roadside birds in some suburban areas, but rare in towns, although an occasional bird is recorded in Yarmouth Cemetery in Kitchener Road. Another unusual bird to turn up in these well-watched Cemeteries is the Water Rail with three recent records. All are obviously migrants possibly attracted by the town lights.

Gulls of several species are regular visitors to towns and villages, including the Lesser Black-backed Gull and Herring Gull. Surprisingly, both these species now nest in Yarmouth and Gorleston on factory roofs or older buildings. A survey in 1999 revealed that at least 31 pairs of Herring Gulls and 12 pairs of Lesser-Black-backs were nesting. Even the scarce, but increasing Mediterranean Gull has been noted feeding on discarded chips in Yarmouth Market place on one occasion. On a similar note, Oystercatchers have also bred recently on flat roofs in Yarmouth at two sites; an unusual practice, but not unknown.

Wood Pigeons and Collared Doves are both common in all suitable habitats while Stock Doves are present in much smaller numbers. Tawny Owls often nest in trees in churchyards and cemeteries or even large wooded gardens and can be heard calling throughout the night. Barn Owls however, are likely to be seen hunting at dusk along roadsides and sadly often become casualties to fast moving cars or lorries.

Swifts are strictly summer visitors to Yarmouth, Gorleston and Caister arriving in mid-May and departing in August. Although they have decreased considerably in recent years, reasonable numbers continue to nest in roofs of older buildings. Favoured areas include Cobholm, Southtown, the Northgate Street area and the Bells Road area of Gorleston. Screaming parties of these birds, often flying low around the houses, are a special feature in July. Although House Martins have finally ceased to nest in Yarmouth town centre, a small colony of these birds has recently become established in Newtown. Others nest in villages, but are nowhere as common as formerly. One particular house in West Somerton held no less than 27 nests in 1974 and since 1991, not a single nesting pair has returned.

Green and Great Spotted Woodpeckers are occasionally attracted to the larger parks and cemeteries, particularly in autumn and winter. Some Great Spotted Woodpeckers are migrants from the Continent and one appeared on Yarmouth Seafront one September, totally exhausted.

Pied Wagtails nest in suitable habitats in towns and villages and this is one species that may possibly be on the increase in numbers. In winter, they form communal roosts, one site used being the James Paget Hospital complex in Gorleston.

People who are fortunate to have cotoneaster shrubs in their gardens or live near a hawthorn hedge, will, in certain years, be favoured by a visit from Waxwings. These winter visitors are irruptive migrants from the forest belts of northern Europe and are easily identifiable by their distinctive crests. Major irruptions occurred in 1965 and 1988 when several hundred Waxwings were in the area. The rather shy Dunnock or Hedge Sparrow as it is often called, is a widespread breeding species present in all areas, numbers being partly increased in autumn by migrants from Europe. The well-known Robin is also abundant, being a resident as well as a passage migrant, breeding freely in gardens, villages and parks. Large arrivals of continental Robins have occurred in several autumns, early October 1998 being of particular note when perhaps as many as five hundred were in evidence along the Yarmouth coastline.

Since 1950, a few pairs of the scarce, but attractive Black Redstart have nested in Yarmouth and Gorleston, mainly in old buildings and industrial areas of the town. The former large South Denes Power Station was a favoured nesting locality and others have nested at the old fishwharf and in the Yarmouth Rows; 1973 was an outstanding year with a record 17-18 pairs rearing at least 50 young. The majority of the males are usually immature, but a few are adult birds complete with their distinctive white wing flashes. In recent years however, fewer breeding birds have been found, possibly due to less suitable sites being available. It is also a passage migrant and is occasionally seen in winter.

The Blackbird needs no introduction and is a very common resident, passage migrant and winter visitor in all areas. Sadly the once common Song Thrush has declined from many garden areas in recent years, but good numbers often arrive in autumn from Scandinavia. Its larger cousin, the Mistle Thrush, is scarcer but surprisingly a pair bred successfully in Yarmouth Cemetery for perhaps the first time in 1999. This site is an ideal location for migrant thrushes on passage and Ring Ouzels are recorded here annually in spring and autumn when favourable winds persist. One of the rarest of all vagrants to occur here was a Red-flanked Bluetail, found by one lucky observer in October 1994. It was the first ever seen in Norfolk and stayed three days, affording excellent views to all who came to admire it.

Many species of warblers also frequent these extensive cemeteries but all are passage migrants. Willow Warblers, Chiffchaffs, Blackcaps and Garden Warblers are among the more regular visitors together with Whitethroats and Lesser Whitethroats. Scarcer species include Wood, Icterine and Yellow-browed Warblers whilst Arctic, Bonelli's and Pallas's Warblers have all been recorded.

Goldcrests appear in autumn, often in large numbers whilst the much scarcer Firecrest is recorded here almost annually. One or two pairs of Spotted Flycatchers nest in the cemeteries and other suitable areas in Yarmouth whilst passage Pied Flycatchers appear on autumn migration. Both Blue and Great Tits are widespread and well known. Coal Tits are scarcer and prefer larger areas with a few adjacent coniferous trees. The Long-tailed Tit is usually seen in gardens in the winter period, but odd pairs will nest where suitable habitat exists.

Magpies have recently invaded towns and urban gardens whilst the shier Jay has recently taken to visiting some of the larger gardens. Rooks and Jackdaws both nest in Yarmouth and recently Carrion Crows have followed the Magpie into many areas. Starlings and House Sparrows are quite abundant, although rather surprisingly, both have experienced population decreases in recent years. Other visitors to town and village gardens include Greenfinch, Goldfinch, Brambling and Linnet, but regular feeding in any garden can produce surprises. One lucky regular feeder in Southtown had a scarce and shy Hawfinch in his backyard for a short period in April 1989.

MAMMALS

The list of mammals to be found in this category is perhaps not as varied as in some other habitats but nevertheless several species are to be found in and around the town.

Some of the antics and shortcomings of the Grey Squirrel have been mentioned in a previous chapter. They are to be found in both St. Georges Park in the town centre and in Priory Gardens in Gorleston where they provide amusement to many folk, especially the children. Both Gorleston and Yarmouth churchyards also have their resident greys as do other wooded areas within or fringing the towns and villages. They are also known to visit many private gardens, perhaps more so today than ever before. They are attracted by the food put out for birds and their cunning and ingenuity permits them to overcome many hurdles utilised to deter them, for they are most persistent when they are attracted to a food source. Many people are unfortunately unaware of the damage they are capable of causing and because of this their ultimate fate may be similar to that of the Coypu.

During recent years there have been many sightings of the Red Fox *Vulpes vulpes* both in and around the town itself. They have been seen along the South Denes around the harbour's mouth, on land to the rear of the Harfrey's Industrial Estate where they have bred and also on Southtown Common. Their earths have also been found at Cobholm, around Caister airfield and around the Caister Road golf course. They are frequently seen on the outskirts of the villages, often at night as they are illuminated by motor car lights. Occasional dead specimens are found as traffic casualties along the main roads leading to and from the town, notably along the new Gorleston by-pass and the Caister by-pass.

In the area of the harbour's mouth, around the piles forming the construction of the famous old pier, Brown Rats *Rattus norvegicus* are occasionally to be seen as they forage for any edible morsels brought in by the tides, for they will devour almost anything be it putrid or pleasant. It has to be said that neither mice nor rats are to be seen in, or around the town as often as they were in the past. The general standard of cleanliness, of both private homes and the town itself, is much better than say a hundred years ago. Sanitation has improved and the use of detergents and other controlling measures has left everywhere cleaner than it might otherwise have been. Within the town itself, the Brown Rat was frequent up to thirty years ago but today a sighting is a far less common occurrence.

Just occasionally a sighting of a Muntjac Deer *Muntiacus reevesi* causes some excitement within the town. A single specimen was actually seen strolling along Englands Lane in Gorleston and another caused a stir when it entered a shop in Yarmouth. These are of course extremely uncommon sightings but they are occasionally seen around the villages, especially on the outskirts. The fact that they are increasing in numbers may provide more sightings such as these in the future.

It is sad indeed that most of the records of the Hedgehog *Erinaceus europaeus* that are received by mammal recorders are of dead specimens that end their lives as road casualties. However, even these records serve to tell us that they are around. They often visit private gardens at night as they hunt for slugs and other small creatures that help to form their diet. Many folk try to encourage them by leaving out saucers of milk, or cat food at night in the hope that they will continue to visit. Should the garden hold an ample stock of their natural food they will almost certainly visit on a regular basis even without encouragement. Hedgehogs feed on a variety of foods which include mice and voles as well as frogs and it may surprise some folk that they will also attack and kill an adder for food. Their spines prevent the adder from biting the flesh and they are able to approach the snake close enough to be able to bite it, a sight that most naturalists would like to witness. They are indeed noisy creatures and when prowling in the garden at night can often be heard as they brush through vegetation in their hunt for food; very often they can be heard grunting as well. Essentially creatures of the night, they are occasionally seen during daylight hours. They are hibernating animals, but during mild winters may often rise and venture abroad. On occasions they may find a quiet corner in the garden in which to spend the winter, perhaps under a pile of leaves or logs. Records have been received of specimens found in gardens as well as several other locations. On one occasion eleven specimens were seen at Liffen's Holiday Park at Burgh Castle at around ten o'clock at night.

One small mammal, although rarely seen, provides us with evidence of its presence throughout the countryside and in the garden. The Mole *Talpa europaea* is a common enough creature and if present in the garden, may cause the keen gardener much concern about his treasured lawn. They are not at all particular where they push up their hills as they tunnel around in their search for food. They feed mainly on worms and other small creatures of the soil but the damage they do in this quest is well known. Occasionally dead specimens are found lying on the ground and during times of flooding in low-lying areas, many are drowned.

Most of the bats to be seen in and around the town are Pipistrelles *Pipistrellus pipistrellus* which are a fairly common sight almost everywhere during the summer, as the daylight fades and night falls. They take gnats and other small flying insects on the wing. They hibernate from October to March in hollow trees, church steeples or towers and even in the roof spaces of private dwellings, sometimes with the more legitimate occupants being unaware of their presence. Other bats may occasionally be seen such as the Noctule Bat *Nyctalus noctula* but for the average person identification is often difficult.

Perhaps the most unusual mammal record to appear within this category is that of an Otter *Lutra lutra* which was found close by the river at Gorleston, near the old ferry site. The creature was captured and released back into the wild in a different location. How it made its way there is not known but its sighting is of great importance. Many have been bred in confinement in recent years and reintroduced into the wild in an attempt to help them re-establish themselves, and to see one locally means that they are managing to survive.

INSECTS

There are of course hundreds of insects of all kinds to be found in the urban habitat, especially in private and public gardens. There are far too many to bring to the attention of the reader in a volume such as this. However, some must be mentioned with regard to this more specialised habit within towns and villages.

The Common Wasp *Vespula vulgaris* for example builds its nest in a variety of places, among them the roof spaces of private dwellings, much to the consternation of the occupants. The queen enters the roof space through the tiniest of holes in early spring with the intention of constructing a starter nest essential in the forming of her colony. She collects wood, which she chews up, mixes with her saliva and moulds into a sphere that she attaches to roof joists or spars. It is in this sphere that she lays her first eggs. As the eggs hatch the young wasps that emerge will often begin to enlarge the structure to allow for expansion of the colony. Sometimes they will abandon the starter nest and begin to construct a new nest elsewhere. As the colony grows the nest increases in size until it is completed. The completed nest of the wasp is indeed a work of art and has to be examined in order to appreciate that fact.

A complete nest may hold two thousand or more wasps thus creating a certain element of risk for the occupants. That number of wasps on the move in and around the house often results in one or more of the occupants being stung. Generally the local pest control officer is called in to deal with the matter.

Various other species of social wasp, or perhaps the Hornet, may at times be encountered or their nest discovered. The Tree Wasp *Dolichovespula sylvestris*, for example, constructs its nest in trees and bushes, a much smaller affair than that of the Common wasp and usually found hanging from a branch. The Red Wasp *Vespula rufa* nests below the ground.

Wherever flowers are seen so are the bumble bees and perhaps one of the earliest to be seen is *Bombus terrestris* sometimes called the Buff-tailed Bumblebee. It visits gardens and parks as well as fields and meadows in the countryside and is extremely common. Another common species is the Common Carder Bee *B. pascuorum* that frequents similar places to *B. terrestris*.

Another bee that may be very common in gardens during spring is the Honey Bee *Apis mellifera*; this species has been kept by bee-keepers for around 6000 years. In the wild they build nests entirely by themselves from start to finish whereas those that adopt hives have had much of the work done for them. They frequent gardens and parks as well as several other habitats and are important pollinators of flowering plants.

It may be of interest to the reader that there is another fairly small bee that is to be found occasionally in the garden; this is the Red Osmia *Osmia rufa*. It has rather different habits to many other bees in the way that it constructs the resting place for its eggs. Sometimes they adopt nesting boxes designed for Blue Tits, cracks in old brickwork or other apertures in buildings and the author has seen them using the small square apertures in an earthenware air brick built in the walls of a bungalow. Other such unlikely places are also utilised. The female will collect soil particles close by the adopted nest site, which she moistens with her saliva, and begin to construct a mud cell in the chosen spot. She will continue until the required number of cells has been constructed and she will lay an egg into each cell. Upon completion she will seal the cells and leave them to their own devices.

Various aphids find a ready home within private and public gardens and cause us some aggravation when they infest our favourite garden plants. Commonly known as greenfly several infest our roses, while others attack various other plants and apart from often eventually killing them, also make them unsightly. Whitefly in greenhouses and scale insects on trees all add to the headaches of the keen gardener. One moth, whose caterpillar may cause havoc among the gooseberries and currant bushes in the garden is the Magpie Moth *Abraxus grossulariata*. Quite a beautiful creature in its own right but its caterpillars may be considered a pest amongst these fruit bushes. The moth is seen on the wing during summer and is indeed quite variable.

Various beetles such as the Violet Ground Beetle *Carabus violaceus* are also present in the urban habitat thanks to gardens and other green areas. This insect usually stays under cover during the daylight hours but at night it ventures out and wages war among the slugs that also seek to feed in the dark.

In recent years the urban habitat has benefited from the fact that many more private gardens have had garden ponds added as a feature. Often built for the pleasure of their owners, to enable them to sit on sunny days watching the fish swimming lazily to and fro, ponds not only provide pleasant viewing for homeowners but also serve to provide a new habitat for many species of wildlife. This is equally true for those ponds in public gardens and, of course, village ponds.

Many of the water creatures are not so restricted to water as one might imagine. As most of the water beetles are equipped with wings and are able to fly, they are always on the lookout for new areas of water where the food supply may be richer than their previous home.

Specimens of the Common Water Beetle *Acilius sulcatus* are often found on paths or driveways beside a car; it seems that in certain lights they mistake the shiny bodywork of a car for water and attempt to drop into it to their detriment. The Great Diving Beetle *Dytiscus marginalis* has been found in similar circumstances; large greenhouses pose a similar problem for them, which is not really surprising.

Several of the dragonflies and damselflies lay their eggs into the stems of aquatic plants and some merely drop them into the water, so the pond-owner may well reap the benefit of providing a home for the larva of these creatures. There may also be the reward in spring or early summer of being able to watch the emergence procedure of a fresh young dragonfly as it makes its entrance into the world that it will share with us for a while. Whilst most folk are used to seeing the adult dragonflies on the wing during summer, not so many are acquainted with their larva, probably because most of their life is spent within the water and they rarely surface. Some species remain in the water for two to three years.

Of course the many and varied flowering plants in any garden whether private or public, will attract hoards of different insects all seeking out the life-giving nectar that may be extracted from such plants. Both insects and plants are all very different in the way that they live their lives but are nevertheless all very dependent on each other for their very survival. In seeking out the nectar the various species of bumble bee, whether inadvertently or not, gather pollen grains on their bodies, spreading them to other plants that they may visit and the great plan of things ensures that each provides a service to the other.

Many of the plants attract their own pests and the pests in turn attract their own predators. Slugs for instance will devour the leaves of many plants with abundant foliage and hedgehogs will seek the slugs as a food source. Aphids will be attracted to roses and many other attractive plants and the larva of many species of hoverflies and ladybirds will in turn be attracted to these little creatures that are so annoying to the gardener. There are numerous other garden pests but there are always creatures that feed on them in order to keep the balance required by nature. This is true, of course, in all wildlife habitats.

Flowering plants in private and public gardens, and of course parks, will attract butterflies, not least of all the Small Tortoiseshell *Aglais urticae* and Peacock *Inachis io* and these most colourful of insects bring a great deal of pleasure and delight to many people. Most of the commoner species are to be found during warm days in summer. Even some of these beautiful creatures occasionally cause some concern to the gardener, especially the vegetable gardener, who of course will detest the visitations of the Large White Butterfly *Pieris brassicae* to his patch. It lays its eggs on plants in the *Brassicaceae* family and when these hatch, the developing caterpillars can quickly cause a great deal of damage to the leaves of such as cabbages and other members of the group. In normal years when the white butterflies are only around in moderate numbers, the damage is probably tolerable but in years when the whites are abundant and the damage is subsequently greater then the vegetable gardener has much to complain about.

The gardener who is keen on encouraging various insects into his garden may well install the plants and shrubs into his garden that are well known for attracting particular species. The butterfly lover will always include species of Buddleias and Ice plants for example.

In recent years there have been several reports of two of the smaller beetles being found in private dwellings. One of these, sometimes called the Fur Beetle *Attagenus pellio*, is bluish black with two white spots on the elytra. They may be found in houses among furs, or actually in carpets, where they lay their eggs and the resulting larvae cause untold damage to such materials. They will also devour stored grains such as rice or wild birdseed. The other beetle is known as the Varied Carpet Beetle *Anthrenus verbasci* and is a bigger pest than the previous species; again it is the larvae that do the damage. Creatures such as these, when discovered, should quickly be dealt with and removed from the house for they will cause great damage to carpets and woollens and if allowed to get a hold are then difficult to eradicate.

There are many other creatures that cause damage within the home in a similar way, various house moths for example are not pests themselves but their larvae are. They are less common today and the use of mothballs is much less frequently seen as a deterrent.

Other green spaces within the urban environment such as churchyards and cemeteries may also be home to a great deal of wildlife. The cemeteries around the Kitchener Road area in Yarmouth for example, because of their geographical position along the coast, often play host, albeit usually for a short period only, to many migrant species arriving here from foreign shores. Every year there are hundreds of dragonflies such as Common Darter *Sympetrum striolatum* and Ruddy Darter *S.sanguineum* seen around the graves, resting from the labours of their journey across the North Sea from the continent. They may be seen all over the cemeteries during late July and August, sometimes hundreds of them, and in other years merely a few dozens. Another species generally seen here is the Migrant Hawker *Aeshna mixta*.

During early August 1995 there was an unexpected influx of dragonflies to the Yarmouth cemeteries, including some species that had not been seen here for many years. Among the hundreds of Common and Ruddy Darters were good numbers of Yellow Winged Darters *S. flaveolum*. As observers took to the cemeteries on the lookout for these beautiful creatures it was soon discovered that there were one or two much rarer species to be found among them. Odd specimens of the Black Darter *S. danae* and the Vagrant Darter *S. vulgatum* were discovered and the news of these species brought dragonfly enthusiasts from all over the country to see them, for the Vagrant Darter had not been seen in Britain since the 1940s.

Various moths and butterflies are also observed here having arrived from abroad. Again during 1995, two or three Camberwell Beauty Butterflies *Nymphalis antiopa* were observed flying around with many would-be photographers in hot pursuit.

During most years there are many hoverflies to be seen within the confines of the cemeteries in Yarmouth and it may be generally supposed that some migration of certain species may take place. Certainly, on occasions, the large numbers of some species would lead the hoverfly student to suspect this to be the case. *Syrphus vitripennis*, *Eristalis tenax* and *Episyrphus balteatus* are among those that may be seen in large numbers for a day or two and then they almost disappear giving the impression that they rested on arrival for a period and then dispersed further inland. Much more study with regard to the migration of hoverflies is required before any firm conclusions can be made as to which species can be considered as true migrants.

The wildlife in and around the villages within our recording area may of course be rather more interesting than that in the town itself due to the outlying rural location of the villages. The town however, as this chapter has shown, is not devoid of some interesting wildlife.

AMPHIBIANS

As previously mentioned in this chapter, ponds are not only a pleasing landscape feature of a garden but are an added asset to wildlife. Aquatic creatures very quickly inhabit new areas of water, however large or small. Frogs and toads as well as newts soon find new ponds and if the necessary elements are present, they may well set up home in a new garden pond. There is nothing more pleasing for new pond-owners than to see a batch of frog spawn floating in their pond in springtime, enabling them to watch at close quarters the development of the adult frog.

Chapter 5 — The Coast and Sea-Shore

THE HABITAT

The British Isles is a collection of islands totalling almost 1,000 in number. It has total length of coastline of nearly 17,000 kilometres (11,000 miles) and it is therefore not surprising that a great deal of wildlife has come to depend on this habitat.

This book deals with just a tiny fraction of that total length of coastline, about 22 kilometres (14 miles) and a correspondingly smaller amount of wildlife. As you read this chapter however you will discover mention of some wildlife that, although nationally very rare, features very strongly on our local coast. For instance the largest breeding colony of Little Terns in the British Isles nests every summer, literally alongside our human visitors, on Yarmouth's own S.P.A. the North Beach.

Most of the coastline between the Hundred Stream at Horsey and Hopton consists of a sandy shoreline backed up by a dune system, sandy cliffs or man-made sea defences. The Winterton dunes are a good example of a typical dunes system consisting of a strip of sandy beach backed by small fore dunes, these in turn graduating to marram stabilised dunes and then even further to coastal heathland, with some low wind scoured areas known as wet slacks. A dunes system is a dynamic system and will, over time, slowly change shape due to the influence of prevailing winds. As early colonising plants die-off and release compost back into the sand so the enriched sand becomes more like soil and the flora and dependant fauna will also change with time.

There are some pebbly beaches such as that of the north beach at Yarmouth; this again is backed by a fairly typical dunes system but is cut short by the sea wall. An expedition from Salisbury to Jellicoe Roads between the sea wall and the tide-line in early summer is an extremely rewarding venture that can be undertaken with minimum preparation and effort. Read on in this chapter and find out why.

Beyond here the beach narrows with very little of interest, apart from the harbour area, until the crumbling sand cliffs between the end of the sea defences at Gorleston and this book's Southern boundary at Hopton.

PLANTS

Probably the most important plant, and the most prolific, along our stretch of the coast from Horsey in the North to Hopton in the South is Marram *Ammophila arenaria*. It forms extensive areas by means of creeping underground stems and in so doing helps to stabilise the dunes. It has been much planted over the years for this purpose.

A very common umbellifer of the coastal strip is Alexanders *Smyrnium olusatrum*. It is probably recorded in all parts of our area but is more profuse by the coast, where it enjoys the less severe winter temperatures. Sea Beet *Beta vulgaris ssp maritima* is a relative of sugar beet and beetroot and grows usually on sandy seashores. The Bluebell *Hyacinthoides spp* which is found in this part of our area is mostly discarded garden plants such as *Hyacinthoides x varibilis*.

Birdsfoot Trefoil *Lotus corniculatus* is frequent on the North Denes creating bright yellow-orange patches when in flower from May to September. Biting Stonecrop *Sedum acre*, which is also known by the alternative name of Wall-pepper from the peppery taste in its short fleshy leaves, is a mass of small star-like flowers from May to July which are unmistakable wherever it grows. White Stonecrop *Sedum alba* which is closely related can be found growing in the same areas.

Another frequent plant of the dunes is Ladies Bedstraw *Gallium verum*, and Sheep's Sorrel *Rumex acetosella*, is also abundant on the acid sandy soils of the coastal dunes. Sorrels are extremely variable in form and hybrids are often produced, which makes identification difficult. Sheepsbit *Jasione Montana*, which is often wrongly called Sheepsbit Scabious, is no relation to the scabious family but is a member of the Bellflower family *Campanulaceae*, and is confined to the short acid turf of the dunes. The leaves are arranged in a spiral pattern around the stem rather than in opposite pairs like a true scabious and the stigma has three lobes instead of two. The bright blue flowering head, which has given it the alternative name of Blue Bonnets, attracts many insect visitors during the flowering season.

Another very attractive plant of this area is the Hare's-foot Clover *Trifolium arvense* which is frequent on the light sandy soils of our coast. The name refers to the soft, downy heads of the flowers which have the shape and texture of a hares foot; this species is no longer common on arable ground but is naturalised on grassy banks and sandy soils.

Sea Bindweed *Convolvulus soldanella*, unlike ordinary bindweed, does not climb and cling to other plants. It only grows in coastal habitats where it trails over the higher areas of the seashore and is abundant on the sand and shingle of the dunes.

Sea Sandwort *Honckenya peploides* grows in extensive carpets of bright, glossy green unlike many seaside plants which are a dull greyish colour. Once the plant is established on sand, and although only a few inches high, it will act as windbreak causing sand to pile up on the windward side creating an embryonic dune. It is a native plant common around this coast and on most of the Denes.

Yellow Rattle *Rhinanthus minor* is also frequent on the sand of the dunes and gets its name from the yellow flowers and the rattling of the ripe seeds in the seedcase. Other plants which thrive in this habitat are Sea Rocket *Cakile maritima* which inhabits the drift line and dune edge and Common Sorrel *Rumex acetosa* which is also very frequent. Sea Holly *Eryngium maritimum* with its striking silver-grey spiky leaves and beautiful blue scented flowers, which emerge in July-August to attract many insects, is also abundant in our area.

Common Restharrow *Ononis repens* is frequent on the established dunes. So folklore tells us it is thus called because on arable land, the tough widespread roots were capable of stopping a horse drawn plough. It is frequently mistaken for Spiny Restharrow *O. spinosa* as it too can have spines.

A very rare plant of this area found only on the North Denes at Yarmouth is Woolly Hawkweed *Hieracium lanatum*, which has become an established garden escape. The only other known site is at Canterbury in Kent (see Alien Plants of the British Isles P315).

Other rarities include Grey Hair-grass *Corynephorus canescens* which is a nationally rare species, very scattered along this coast, and only abundant on the sand dunes between Winterton and Yarmouth.

Lesser Meadow-rue *Thalictrum minus*, although nationally quite rare, can still be found on the sand dunes near Caister Golf Course where it has persisted for more than a hundred years.

Quite a number of garden escapes, which seem to be discarded plants from houses along Marine Parade, can be found along the sea wall backing the sand dunes. Among these are Butterfly Bush *Buddleia davidii*, Sweet Alison *Lobularia maritima*, Pink Sorrel *Oxalis articulata*, Larkspur *Consolida ajacis*, Rose Campion *Lychnis coronaria*, Snapdragon *Antirrhinum majus* and Snow-in-summer *Cerastium tomentosum*.

Other plants found here, although not primarily plants of the seaside habitat, will include Bittersweet, *Solanum dulcamara*, also known as Woody Nightshade, Curled Dock *Rumex crispus* and Common Cleavers or Goosegrass *Galium aperine*.

BIRDS

Starting in the north, the relatively quiet sandy beaches between Horsey Gap and Winterton Ness are home in summer to a small colony of Little Terns. These are protected by English Nature but unfortunately often with little success. Several pairs of Ringed Plovers also breed and in 1967 a pair of common terns nested at Winterton Ness.

In autumn and early winter, sea watching here, particularly during periods of strong northerly winds, can be productive. Leach's Petrels together with Sooty, Balearic and Manx Shearwaters have all been recorded. High totals of migrating wildfowl, particularly Brent Geese, are seen in October and November. Spectacular numbers of Little Auks, all moving north, are also on record. Guillemots are regularly seen, as are Razorbills, particularly in late summer.

The dune system here is extensive and Stonechats breed in very small numbers. The Red Backed Shrike was a common breeding species until the mid 1970s, but it occurs here now only as a migrant. Skylarks and Meadow Pipits are still relatively common and one pair of Woodlarks recently bred. In winter the sandy beaches are given over to groups of Sanderlings and numerous gulls.

Further south, between Winterton village and Hemsby, the wide beaches and dune system continue. Little Terns occasionally nest here but disturbance is often high. Between the dune system and the beginning of the cliffs both Stonechats and Yellowhammers breed in the valley. Migrant birds are regularly looked for here and some unusual finds have been made.

The low cliffs of Scratby and California have recently been colonised by a small colony of Fulmars. These bred successfully for the first time in 1998. Sand Martins also nest here in varying numbers.

Caister sea wall is a popular place from which to sea watch and often both Turnstone and Sanderling are present on the beach and on the sea defences. A small party of Snow Buntings often winters here. To the south of the village Little Terns and Ringed Plovers, although now much disturbed, often frequent the wide sandy beach.

Just inland, the Caister Golf course is the last remnant of the famed Yarmouth North Denes. Here Linnets, Skylarks and Meadow Pipits breed among the "greens". Earlier naturalists recorded Wheatear, Whinchat and Red Backed Shrike nesting here and in recent years both Stonechat and Yellowhammer have ceased to breed here. Although often disturbed by golfers, a few interesting migrants have been recorded including Firecrest, Hoopoe, Barred Warbler and Wryneck.

A little further South is Yarmouth North beach with extensive areas of marram grass. This is now a protected area and is home in summer to the country's largest Little Tern colony. Up to 240 pairs nest here protected by the RSPB and breeding success is varied. Predation by foxes and Kestrels is high, but thanks to 24-hour wardening, results have improved. An information hut supplies the general public with all the latest news and excellent views can be obtained from

Little Tern Chicks

outside the fence of both adults and chicks. Ringed Plovers also nest here and since 1998 a pair of Oystercatchers have bred. In the marram grass areas, Skylarks and Meadow Pipits continue to nest despite the ever-increasing human pressure.

Sea watching here can produce exciting results in stormy weather and both Manx and Sooty Shearwaters can be expected in certain weather conditions in autumn. Leach's Petrels have been seen and in October 1975 several Storm Petrels were observed. The most likely of the Skuas to be seen is the Arctic Skua although the Great Skua is an annual visitor and has been recorded in every month.

The offshore sandbank of Scroby Sands lies almost opposite the Brittannia Pier at Yarmouth. Now covered by virtually every high tide at low tide it stretches a considerable distance from north to south and is constantly changing shape. Scroby Sands forms a natural breakwater to Yarmouth and it hosts a large population of roosting birds on occasions. Terns formerly nested here when it remained dry at high tide between 1947 and 1965 with varied success. During this period, up to 368 pairs of Common Terns, 430 pairs of Sandwich Terns and 27 pairs of Little Terns bred here. A temporary build up of the sandbank again between 1972 and 1976 resulted in up to 56 pairs of Common Terns and 15 pairs of Little Terns nesting again. Since then the sandbank has been covered by most tides.

Yarmouth seafront and particularly the area between the two piers is the best place in Norfolk to see Mediterranean Gulls. Over twenty have been recorded in recent years and groups of adults and immatures are often seen resting on the beach near the jetty.

Moving south, the former open Yarmouth South Denes is now an Industrial area, but small neglected areas persist here and there. These attract groups of Snow Buntings in winter and occasionally a party of Shore Larks will turn up at migration time. A pair of Ringed Plovers attempted to nest here in 1999.

The harbour entrance is an ideal sea watching point and on occasions Purple Sandpipers frequent the weed covered harbour workings just inside the entrance. Turnstones and Sanderlings are more frequent here and Eiders are occasionally seen. This area was formerly good for large numbers of gulls, but since the sewage outlet was closed, the numbers have decreased considerably. Iceland Gull, Glaucous Gull and Sabine's Gull have all been recorded here.

On the Gorleston side to the south of the resort the cliffs are home to a small colony of Sand Martins whilst the adjacent Gorleston golf course is an ideal location for tired migrants, affording plenty of cover. Nesting birds are fewer due to continual disturbance but Linnets and Meadow Pipits are among the more regular. Offshore in winter Eiders and Common Scoter are regular in Gorleston Bay and up until the 1970s, small numbers of Long Tailed Ducks visited nearly every year.

To the south of Hopton and towards the county boundary, the open fields and scrub are well watched by bird watchers. Many unusual migrants have been seen here amongst the more regular birds. Indeed, the first Pine Bunting for Norfolk was identified here in October 1975, a superb find for two local bird watchers.

MAMMALS

The list of mammals found along the coast is not a long one and relies largely on seal records. Occasionally Common Seals *Phoca vitulina* are seen off the foreshore and once in a while they are found ashore; a record exists of a specimen being seen at Horsey during 1998. Pups were born on Caister Beach in 1998 with two pups still present in September.

The Grey Seal *Halychoerus grypus* is known to breed between Horsey and Winterton with 17 pups being born in 1997. The Bird and Mammal report for 1998 states that one died soon after birth, and one well-grown pup was discovered dead with no visible wounds. The remaining 15 left the beach by the second week of January. The colony, of course, attracts a great deal of interest and deservedly so. Careful observation has to be undertaken on a regular basis to monitor the situation and record its progress.

INSECTS

Many insects that are to be seen along the coast may not be strictly termed as coastal species. At times there are to be seen large influxes of migrant insects arriving here from abroad especially during spring and early summer. During July 1992 there was a large influx of migrant butterflies seen arriving from the sea. They were mainly specimens of the Large White Butterfly *Pieris brassicae* although mixed in with these were lots of Small Whites *Artogeia rapae* and smaller numbers of Green-veined Whites *Artogeia napi* and there were even some Small Tortoiseshells *Aglais urticae*. As they flew in there must have been millions of them giving the appearance of a snowstorm along the beach in all directions. This influx continued for around four days and extended from Pakefield in the south to Hemsby in the north: it would be impossible to say just how many may have arrived.

During 1995 there were lots of migrant dragonflies that arrived in the same way and were later found in the Yarmouth cemeteries causing lots of excitement for local enthusiasts. These are listed in more detail in the chapter on the urban habitat.

Along the North Denes at Yarmouth close by where the Little Terns have bred for several years, several species of butterflies have been recorded. The Common Blue *Polyommatus icarus* finds the Birds-foot Trefoil *Lotus corniculatus* growing there to its liking, or at least its caterpillars do, and several specimens have been recorded on a regular basis. Skippers both Large *Ochlodes venatus* and Small *Thymelicus flavus* have been recorded. Graylings *Hipparchia semele* are also to be found, in sometimes greater numbers, further along the coast between Yarmouth and Winterton and are often seen in fairly good numbers throughout August.

The Dark Green Fritillary *Mesoacidalia aglaja* is also to be seen regularly along the coastal dunes between Horsey and Winterton, a habitat greatly to its liking although it also likes more open countryside.

Of course other species of butterflies may generally be seen along the coast although they may not be normally associated with this habitat other than merely passing through. Small Tortoiseshells, Painted Ladies and the whites are usually to found on occasions in almost any kind of habitat.

Many of the migrant insects undoubtedly arrive at night and escape observation on their arrival, for unlike birds arriving at night, insects cannot be recognised by their calls as they pass overhead for they are usually silent.

One of the regular insects that may be associated legitimately with the coast is the Leaf-cutter Bee *Megachile maritima* sometimes called the Coast Leaf-cutter. It alights on various plants and carefully but quickly cuts out a semi-circular section of the leaf, about half an inch in diameter, with its sharp mandibles. This leaf segment is then carried to the spot where it has decided to locate the nest and rolled up into a cigar shaped tube. It is filled with nectar and pollen and an egg is then laid inside the tube and another segment of leaf is used to seal up the end of the tube. The tube is placed into the nesting hole and other tubes are constructed and placed on top of the first. These tubes are then left to their own devices. The process is such that the last egg laid is the first to hatch and the larva eats its way through the nectar and pollen and makes its way out to freedom as an adult bee. The second cell, on hearing the movement of the first, does the same and so on. If however one grub should die then the rest behind it never emerge. Males are the first to emerge and they await the females in order to mate.

The Red-banded Sand Wasp *Ammophila sabulosa* may also be found here in the sand dunes along the coast. They pounce on unwary caterpillars and their sting paralyses them but does not cause their death. The wasp carries the caterpillar to its prepared tunnel in the sand where it lays eggs on and around the hapless creature. The youngsters on hatching are obviously on the lookout for food and the live, but paralysed, caterpillar provides their first meal. They are found almost anywhere where there are sandy conditions and are particularly frequent on Belton Common.

REPTILES

During early spring on pleasant warm and sunny mornings casual dog-walkers need to take care where they walk for this is the time when Adders *Vipera berus* emerge from their winter hibernation and bask in the warm sunshine. Being ectothermic, their body temperature varying with and being dependent on the temperature of the environment, they need to attain sufficient body warmth in order to move properly and to be able to search for food. While they are basking they are fairly dormant and should a dog surprise them they tend to strike more from instinct than savagery and many a dog has required quick attention from the local vet as a result.

FISH

There are many spots along the coast that hold special attractions to shore anglers. At night during the winter months, their lanterns may be seen along the foreshore from some distance away lighting up their chosen space as they do their utmost to tempt the various species of fish from their native element. All kinds of tackle is used in the quest to lure the fish from the deep providing the angler the opportunity to exploit his natural hunting instincts. It has to be said that angling along the coast is not what it used to be and to some extent the blame may be laid at the door of pollution. If the pollution around the coast does not deter the fish themselves, it is very likely that the food that those fish feed on is deterred from venturing too close to our mucky shores. The favourite quarry of the anglers is undoubtedly the Codfish *Gadus morhua*, and anglers will try to out-do each other with the size of the cod that they catch from late October through to around February. Prior to the arrival of the Cod most will settle for the Whiting *Merlangius merlangus*. A good bag of Whitings will provide a family with a worthwhile meal for perhaps a couple of days.

Many anglers will have come to realise that more fish are caught by those who have the technique of casting their lines further out from the shore where the pollution is perhaps a little less concentrated; others overcome these problems by fishing from boats further out past the breakers.

Eels *Anguilla Anguilla*, Bass *Dicentrarchus labrax*, Dabs *Limanda limanda*, Flounder *Platichthys flesus*, and occasionally Soles *Solea solea* may also be taken by the shore angler. One fish that the angler has little interest in catching is the Lesser Weaver *Echiichthys vipera*. The dorsal fin of this formidable looking creature is extremely venomous, as are the spines on its gill covers. The experienced angler knows well the pain that this creature can inflict but an unsuspecting novice may well be caught out and contact with the venomous spines will cause much swelling and extreme pain for sometimes several days. Usually one encounter with the species is enough and a painful lesson is promptly learned. Old hands at angling generally show the creature respect but the head of the creature usually ends up between the ground and the heel of the anglers boot.

Chapter 6 — Inland Fresh Water

THE HABITAT

Around the Yarmouth area there are not many areas of true freshwater; the Broads for example vary in their degrees of salinity depending upon the tidal movements. At times of higher tides the saline waters are carried further toward the higher reaches and into several of the broads and, consequently, creatures that are able to withstand only a small degree of salinity are not always to be found in the Broads system. It is of course true to say that many of the creatures that are found in marshland, would also be found in and around freshwater ponds and lakes. Dragonflies for example would be found in both habitats. The same could be said of many other insects and, of course, some of the fishes.

Fritton Lake and Lound Waterworks are the largest areas of true freshwater to be found within the area and neither are worked on a regular basis in order to determine the species to be found in their waters, due to their being privately owned. There are other much smaller areas of freshwater such as farm ponds, even garden ponds that may provide much of great interest to the student of freshwater biology but these are seldom available for study. In the Hopton House estate in the village of Hopton to the south of Gorleston, there is an extensive pond of around two and a half acres which for many years, was recorded extensively on a regular basis. This area of water is connected to the reservoirs in the Lound Waterworks system and a great deal of the wildlife found at the waterworks may also be found on this estate. Despite its title, much of the area of the waterworks falls within the Hopton boundaries and consequently lies within the recording area covered by this book. Angling is not generally permitted in the waterworks although employees of the Water Company are at times given leave to fish the waters. It has not been possible to survey the waters to any great extent in order to give a true picture of the aquatic life but the author has accumulated a number of records over many years that may prove helpful. A number of accounts of fish captured have come from those that have fished the waters legitimately and some from unauthorised anglers and the records show that some fair sized fish have at times been taken.

Usually when gravel workings are opened up there is a public outcry from folks living in the area concerned about the noise, lorries continually passing their homes and indeed other factors that may cause anxiety. This is of course a matter of great concern for all involved but it has to be said that when the workings later become redundant, with careful and considerate management they may become places of great beauty and provide a completely new wildlife habitat. This has happened in many places throughout Britain and many folk are now able to appreciate these new habitats.

These workings leave enormous hollows in the ground. They are eventually filled naturally with water and over a period of several years mature with all kinds of wildlife taking up residence. Birds are probably the first colonisers and inadvertently carry seeds either attached to their bodies or in their digestive systems, to the edges of these pits. Consequently plants start to grow around the margins and if allowed to grow naturally, they soon spread in favourable conditions. The eggs of various fish are often transported in the same way. Sometimes these gravel pits are very deep becoming home to certain species of fish like the Pike, Carp and Tench and, of course, wherever large fish are to be found, another species usually follows, the angler. Several of the local gravel pits have been stocked with larger specimens as an attraction and anglers are charged fees for the privilege of fishing the waters. Many anglers today prefer to fish gravel pits rather than the rivers for when they sit beside a pit they are at least certain that there are fish in front of them whereas in the rivers there may be no fish in the vicinity for hours on end.

PLANTS

The Broads, local ponds, the edges of rivers, dykes and ditches including Lound Ponds (Water Works) are our main areas of fresh water and many of the plants are the same as those recorded in the marshland areas. The characteristic trees are species such as Alder *Alnus glutinosa* a very common tree of the Yarmouth area found in carr, lakesides such as Lound, river banks and many damp woods. In fact this tree thrives in wet ground, it is recognized by its regular branching and conical shape and grows to 70ft. (22m). The leaves are alternate, rounded and very often notched at the tips while the buds are stalked. Male and female catkins grow on the same tree, ripening in the spring, the ripe fruits staying on the tree throughout the winter.

The twigs of the Crack Willow *Salix fragilis* are very brittle and can be broken off at a joint between branch and twig very easily hence the Latin name *fragilis*. This brittleness has served the willow in good stead through the years, as it has allowed it to spread itself far afield. As this tree grows near or beside a river so many of these broken twigs will fall and be carried off by the river to lodge on mud where they will take root and grow into new trees. One of the best sites to see the pollarded willow is along the Stokesby Road.

White Willow *S. alba* is another species that is very common to this area although in the last two decades with road widening and bypasses many of our willows have disappeared, including the once prominent Cricket Bat Willow, most of these being the variety *S. alba var. caerulea*.

Common Reed *Phragmites australis* is widespread and locally abundant and can be found in nearly all habitats connected with water (and sometimes without). This is Britain's tallest grass, and that grown on the Norfolk Broads has become synonymous with thatching. The plant's huge feathery heads stand erect, but will start to droop as the seeds ripen.

Water Fern *Azolla filiculoides* is a small but highly gregarious floating fern, which occurs on many of the dykes and ponds in the area. Dense stands exclude almost all competitors; less dense aggregations are often mixed with Duckweeds.

White Water-Lily *Nymphaea alba*, often grows in abundance in still water on the Norfolk Broads, ponds, dykes and ditches in the area. It is usually found at depths of half to one-and-a-half metres in open water, but it can grow in very shallow water. It is notably intolerant of disturbed water. Where water in the area has become polluted it has been noticed that it soon disappears.

Yellow Water-Lily *Nuphar lutea* is a plant of slow-flowing rivers, ponds and dykes. It is normally found in open water at depths of half to two-and-a-half metres but has been recorded deeper. It over winters as a rhizome, producing submerged leaves in early spring and leather like floating leaves in April and May. It flowers from June to August.

Common Water Starwort *Callitriche stagnalis* inhabits the edges of rivers, ponds, dykes and ditches. It can also be found growing on moist or disturbed ground such as wheel ruts or where cattle have trodden, tracks, woodland rides and occasionally arable fields.

The floating rosettes of Frog-bit *Hydrocharis morsus-ranae* are normally found in shallow water such as the broads, ponds, ditches and dykes. It is a herbaceous perennial now becoming scarce outside the Broads area. This plant which grows in still water faces a problem of survival in a harsh British winter. The first method of securing survival is to produce seeds that sink to the bottom of the pond in autumn and there develop into young plants; these rise to the surface in the spring. The other method is to grow special winter buds, which sink to the bottom in the comparatively warm mud. Here they remain dormant until the warmth of the spring gives them the signal to grow into tiny plantlets that float up to the surface and begin a new growing season.

NATURE IN EAST NORFOLK

(39) Lesser Celandine

(40) Canadian Fleabane

(41) Hedgehog

(42) Wasps' Nest in House Rafters

(43) Peacock Butterfly

NATURE IN EAST NORFOLK

(44) Magpie Moth

(45) Garden Spider

(46) Yellow-winged Darter

NATURE IN EAST NORFOLK

(47) North Beach S.P.A. from the Air

(48) The North Beach S.P.A. in Early Summer

Two members of the orchid family that have been recorded in the Lound area are Common Twayblade *Listera ovata* and Early Purple Orchid *Orchis mascula*. Neither have been prolific with the Early Purple Orchid preferring heavier soil than is usual in our area and the Common Twayblade is now absent.

BIRDS

The many rivers, streams, broads and ponds together with a few flooded gravel pits in the area form a great variety of habitats for birds. Little Grebes breed in secluded areas in summer, but are more obvious in winter as they move onto larger stretches of water. The attractive Great Crested Grebe has decreased as a breeding bird in the recorded area especially on the four Flegg Broads (Filby, Ormesby, Rollesby and Lily). In 1961, there were 125 adults here in the summer, but a survey in 1998 revealed that only a total of eight adults were present. The reason behind this decrease is unknown and is against the county and national trend, which shows a healthy increase. The population on Fitton Lake and the adjacent Lound Waterworks appears to be stable. The remaining species of grebe, Red-necked, Slavonian and Black-necked are all scarce winter visitors, more likely to be seen in very harsh and cold conditions. Cormorants are likely to be seen on any sizeable stretch of water and have increased considerably since the early 1970's. Many now roost here at certain times of the year. At first light birds fly out to feed on various broads, rivers and streams. Most of these birds, if not all, are considered likely to be of the continental tree nesting race *sinensis*, and are more likely to feed inland.

Bitterns are rarely seen these days, but they have bred in the area on occasions, particularly in the more reedy sections of the lower River Bure between Yarmouth and Acle and at Ormesby Broad. Martham Broad apart, the last breeding pairs were recorded in 1984, and since then the species has declined nationally. Grey Herons are still a relatively common sight in most localities, the largest breeding heronry being at Burgh Castle. One or two other small colonies exist, but several former sites such as the one at Mautby Decoy have long been abandoned.

The Mute Swan needs no introduction as it is one of the most obvious birds on the broads, rivers and lakes. Large numbers sometimes gather at riverside staithes to be fed by holidaymakers. In recent years, feral Black Swans have made an appearance in the area. An Australian species and slightly smaller than the Mute Swan, no less than five together were seen on Fritton Lake in May 1998.

Feral Greylag Geese and Canada Geese are now present in substantial numbers on the Flegg Broads, in the vicinity of Martham Broad and on Fritton Lake, whilst smaller numbers of feral Barnacle Geese are often seen at the latter site. To complicate, matters one of the presumed feral Barnacle Geese has now been identified (by its ring numbers on its leg) as a genuine wild individual which was ringed in Sweden in 1989. It bred at Fritton Lake for the first time in 1998 with a presumed feral bird and reared five goslings.

Shelducks breed in small numbers not too far from the coast, favouring areas in the mid-Waveney Valley, particularly between Belton and Somerleyton. In winter, all migrate to coastal areas and feed on estuaries. Ducks are numerous as expected in such habitats, the Mallard is common and widespread on virtually all open spaces of water and ponds. Other species of dabbling (surface feeding) ducks include Gadwall, Teal and Shoveler, whilst Wigeon favour marshes and Pintail estuarine habitats; The Garganey, a summer visitor, is unusual. Of the diving ducks, the more obvious are Pochards and Tufted Ducks whilst Goldeneyes appear on larger stretches of water. Rarer ducks could possibly include more marine species such as Scaup, Common Scoter and Long-tailed Duck. In severe wintry weather the attractive Smew and Goosander are worth looking out for. Recently, certainly since 1979, a few Ruddy Ducks have appeared in the area and a pair bred successfully at Mautby Decoy in 1998.

Birds of prey in this type of habitat are less common, but it is home to the Marsh Harrier. Reed beds alongside broads and rivers are its chief habitat and several pairs now breed in the area thanks to protection. It is not unusual to see several together and with milder winters, a few birds now stay throughout the year. The fish eating Osprey is always possible on larger open areas of water between April and early October; all are passage birds, many presumably of Scandinavian origin.

Coots and Moorhens are reasonably abundant in watery areas whilst Water Rails may still possibly breed in one or two remote locations. A few arrive in the autumn to winter with us, but being shy birds, are much more likely to be heard than actually seen.

Of the wading birds one of the more likely to be seen is the Common Sandpiper feeding along the edges of streams, rivers and ponds whilst Snipe are often in the same environment. Little Ringed Plovers are possible visitors between April and September on the few flooded gravel pits in the area and odd pairs have attempted to breed on occasions. Dry summers often lead to exposed muddy margins around the broads, lakes and ponds and other wading species are always possible. For example, a juvenile Red-necked Phalarope spent all day at Freethorpe village pond on 4th September 1975 and during the long dry autumn of 1976, up to 6 Greenshank fed daily at Lound Waterworks.

Gulls habitually frequent these areas, the most obvious being the Black-headed Gull, but it is worth looking out for other species. Herring Gulls, Lesser Black-backed Gulls and Common Gulls are all reasonably common, while passage Little Gulls can occasionally appear in spring and autumn. Common Terns breed on specially constructed platforms at both Martham and Ormesby Broads, but feeding birds can turn up almost anywhere. Easterly winds in May could produce parties of Black Terns heading back to their breeding grounds in Holland while occasional birds are also seen in autumn. Other terns that could just possibly be present are Sandwich and Little Terns, both marine species, which occasionally are forced to fish inland due to strong offshore winds. Of the real rarities, Caspian Terns have appeared on Martham Broad on two occasions and on Filby Broad on three occasions in recent years, but great luck is needed to see them.

Large groups of hunting Swifts, Swallows, House Martins and Sand Martins often feed over open water if the weather is bad, but some are usually present on most days. Kingfishers are now certainly scarcer than they have been, but odd pairs still breed in suitable locations. Late summer and autumn is often a good time to see them. Since colonising East Anglia in 1973, Cetti's Warblers are now established in the area at one or two sites, the loud, but short song easily giving away their presence. In the reeds and sedge areas, Reed and Sedge Warblers abound in summer whilst the Grasshopper Warbler is more at home in the more scrubby areas of reed and sedge beds. Bearded Tits are the real specialities of the reed bed and pairs breed around Martham Broad and in the lower Waveney Valley. In autumn and winter, parties move about and any areas of reed could prove attractive to a Bearded Tit. Another reed specialist is the Reed Bunting, a fairly common resident in all waterside areas, it is also a passage migrant and winter visitor despite numbers decreasing in recent years. A few Reed Buntings have also been noted on garden bird tables especially those close to water.

MAMMALS

In our area there are several gravel pits that provide special interest for both the angler and naturalist alike. Green's pits at Burgh Castle is perhaps the most popular one for the anglers, but the naturalist will also find a great deal of interest.

After a spell of fishing many of the anglers may well have some of their bait left over and rather than take it home with them they may throw the remainder into the water or throw it along the banks for the ducks. Often it lies there for some time and occasionally attracts rats which are always willing to clean up anything of an edible nature. Some of the rats here are indeed large specimens, they are not often seen but occasionally they venture out when the lure of food proves tempting.

In the past it was not uncommon while sitting still, engaged in a spot of angling to see a Water Shrew *Neomys fodiens* venture out to seek food but today they are seen far less often. There is much concern about their gradual reduction in numbers and they are being monitored on a regular basis under the auspices of the Norfolk Wildlife Trust in order to determine their status throughout the area. It seems so sad that many of our most engaging creatures are being lost for whatever reason; they all have a purpose to serve within the bounds of nature. Much of the blame for the loss of this creature is being put at the door of the American Mink *Mustela vison* and it makes one's mind return to the fact that this creature is merely another introduction to Britain that has once again upset the balance of nature. The species is to be found around Lound Waterworks and in certain areas around the River Waveney. It's regular appearance in the Norfolk Mammal Report sadly serves to tell us that they have become a breeding species in the wild, for as well as those specimens that are brought to our notice, there must also be many that are not recorded.

Both the Weasel *Mustela nivalis* and the Stoat *M. erminea*, are to be found around Lound Waterworks and Green's Pits as well as many other freshwater areas but are more likely to occur in more open habitats frequently away from water.

Bats are occasionally seen flying over the water at Lound and the species usually identified is the Pipistrelle *Pipistrellus pipistrellus*. This species is our smallest bat and is likely to be seen at dusk flying over any area of freshwater as it seeks out the low flying insects. The Noctule Bat *Nyctalus noctula* also occurs over water at dusk and has been recorded around some of the broads.

Mention should be made here of the Otter *Lutra lutra* although records received have been generally unconfirmed, with the exception of one found by the riverside at Gorleston on the 18th December 1999. Otters are being bred in captivity and when the specimens are mature enough to fend for themselves they are being released into the wild and the sighting of them on inland freshwaters is not out of the question, especially when the area of water is close by the river. Anglers and riverside observers should remain vigilant.

INSECTS

In this kind of habitat it is not surprising that many of the insects to be found are aquatic. However in order to observe them, some indulgence in netting is required. For those with an interest in this kind of pastime, some species that are to be encountered are listed.

There are numerous small crustaceans to be found such as Freshwater Shrimps *Gammarus pulex* and the Water Slater *Asellus aquaticus*; both are extremely common. Water bugs abound such as the Water Boatmen *Notonecta glauca* and Lesser Water Boatmen *Corixa punctata*. During the summer, in quiet weedy corners, one may see the Common Pondskater *Gerris lacustris* as it glides along the surface of the water ever on the lookout for smaller insects that have come to grief. The Water Cricket *Velia caprai* may also be seen lurking in a similar manner, though perhaps a little less common than the previous species. Within the water other bugs lurk; creatures like the Water Scorpion *Nepa cinerea* and the Saucer Bug *Ilyocris cimicoides*, both being ferocious predators on other smaller creatures. The much scarcer Water Stick Insect *Ranatra linearis* has been recorded from Lound

Waterworks, one or two dykes on the Haddiscoe Marshes, (just within our area) and dykes at Horsey. As yet they have not been found at Fritton Lake although it has possibly been overlooked there. There are several water beetles to be found by those that take the trouble to search for them. Probably the largest of these is the Great Diving Beetle *Dytiscus marginalis* which not only attacks other small aquatic insects but will also attack smaller fish fry and delights in young tadpoles during spring and early summer. It is highly predatorial and extremely ferocious in both its adult and nymphal stages. The Common Water Beetle *Acilius sulcatus* has very shiny elytra appearing almost black in colour and is also, as it name suggests, fairly common in the area. Few folk can have failed to notice the Whirlygig Beetle *Gyrinus natator*; this creature has been described elsewhere but is common in this area.

A great deal of angling is carried on at many of the freshwater venues including Fritton Lake. Boats are hired out for the use of anglers and at times good catches are taken. Most anglers like to get amongst the large shoals of Bream and some catches of quite large fish are made. Very few anglers examine the fish that they catch, being quite satisfied to have taken the fish at all. A close inspection of several species will often reveal the tiny Fish Louse *Argulus foliaceus*. Although commonly referred to as a louse, it is not a louse at all but is a crustacean. Its habits though are similar to those of many lice for they feed on the blood of their host. These creatures are more common than may be supposed and are found on quite a number of fish species. Carp, Tench, Pike, Perch, Bream and Dace are all species that may be parasitised and even the Minnows and Sticklebacks are not immune from their attentions. The *Argulus* attaches itself to the fish by means of large suckers on the under side of its body and when attached is held firmly in place. Sometimes many may be seen on a single fish and during a heavy infestation it is not difficult to imagine the fate of the fish. Upon the demise of the host, the creatures release their hold on the victim and swim around freely in search of another host.

Where there are flowering plants to be found growing around these areas of water, butterflies and other nectar seeking insects may be found. There are of course insects that are merely found in or close by watery habitats. Mayflies, for example are to be seen in abundance on occasions. There are in excess of forty species known in Britain although one of the commonest and more likely to be encountered is *Ephemera danica*. Many Mayflies have been given common names by anglers who make imitations in order to attract certain species of fish. This species and several others are to be found in many areas.

There are also several species of Caddis Flies although no particular study into the status of each species appears to have been carried out and the records available are of the observations of a single member. Occasionally the species *Phryganea grandis* may have been seen resting in the crevices of bark on some trees and has also been found at night. It is the largest British Caddis Fly and breeds in slow moving or still water. It has been recorded at Lound Waterworks, Green's Pits at Burgh Castle and Hall Farm Fisheries, also at Burgh Castle. Probably the most commonly encountered species is *Limnephilus flavicornis*. This species is to be found breeding on small ponds and has also been found in marsh dykes. It has been recorded at Lound Waterworks, in odd dykes along the Belton and Burgh Castle marshes and occasionally on the Haddiscoe mashes. *Anabolia nervosa* is also another fairly common species and has been recorded in most of the above mentioned locations. There are many other Caddis Fly species and there is certainly room for much more study into the group.

Dragonflies and damselflies are always associated with water and throughout the region we may encounter as many as twelve species of dragonfly and eight species of damselfly. Considering the total number of species to be found in Britain, those found within our area present a respectable proportion. This is an extremely interesting group of insects and is well worthy of the casual observer devoting a little more time in watching the various species. Contrary to common belief, they are not in any way harmful to humans, they do not bite or sting, as has been suggested, and a little time spent in observing their habits will be more than repaid by being able to understand them a little better. They will often visit even fairly small garden ponds and may even lay their eggs, thus providing the owner with the possibility of being able to see them emerge the following season.

A short list of the species and their rarity value is shown below.

The larger dragonflies

Southern Hawker	Aeshna cyanea	Common	Most areas
Brown Hawker	Aeshna grandis	Common	Most areas
Norfolk Hawker	Aeshna isosceles	Frequent	Broads & Marshes
Migrant Hawker	Aeshna mixta	Common	Most areas
Emperor Dragonfly	Anax imperator	Frequent	Ponds and Lakes
Hairy Dragonfly	Brachytron pratense	Common	Most areas
Blacktailed Skimmer	Orthetrum cancellatum	Common	Ponds and Lakes
Broad-bodied Chaser	Libellula depressa	Occasional	More open areas
4-spotted Chaser	Libellula quadrimaculata	Frequent	Open waters
Scarce Chaser	Libellula fulva	Occasional	River Waveney
Ruddy Darter	Sympetrum sanguineum	Common	Most areas
Common Darter	Sympetrum striolatum	Common	Most areas

The smaller dragonflies

Branded Demoiselle	Calopteryx splendens	Occasional	Odd locations
Emerald Damselfly	Lestes sponsa	Frequent	Most areas
Red-eyed Damselfly	Erthromma najas	Occasional	Odd locations
Large-red Damselfly	Pyrrhosoma nymphula	Common	Most areas
Blue-tailed Damselfly	Ischnura elegans	Common	Most areas
Common Blue Damselfly	Enallagma cyathigerum	Common	Most areas
Azure Damselfly	Coenagrion puella	Common	Most areas
Variable Damselfly	Coenagrion pulchellum	Occasional	Odd locations

REPTILES AND AMPHIBIANS

In warm sunny mornings around the banks of inland freshwaters, a quiet watcher may come upon the Grass Snake *Natrix natrix* basking in the warm sunshine, gently warming itself in preparation for all that the new day brings. Frogs form the greater part of their diet and occasionally the dreadful scream of a frog being taken by a grass snake may be heard; it is indeed a pitiful sound. Small mammals are occasionally also taken as food. Grass Snakes have been recorded from several locations including Lound Waterworks and around the banks of Fritton Lake.

The Common Frog *Rana temporaria* is no longer as common in the wild as it once used to be, however it may still be found in small numbers in ponds and lakes and some of the broads. The same may be said of the Common Toad *Bufo bufo* though this species is less often found than the common frog.

The Common or Smooth Newt *Triturus vulgaris* is quite common in well vegetated ponds and lakes especially during early spring when they take to the water for the purpose of mating and breeding. Contrary to general belief this species does not spend all of its time in water, it usually leaves the water after it has finished mating and egg laying and returns the following spring. The Great Crested Newt *T.cristatus* is far less common than *T. vulgaris* although where it is found it may appear to be quite abundant.

Common Frog

A WORD OF CAUTION

Many households have a freshwater aquarium with various species of fish and no doubt they provide a great attraction to the whole family. Sometimes these aquaria are purchased for youngsters as gifts and they provide amusement for a time but as they grow older the novelty sometimes wears off and the whole system becomes a nuisance with the constant need for cleaning and maintenance. On occasions folk have merely tipped the contents of their aquarium into a pond or other area of freshwater, sometimes with dire consequences. Occasionally these aquaria contain tiny specimens of the catfish and while small, even though they are highly predatorial, they may not cause too much of a problem, but in the wild they can grow to huge dimensions and there have occasionally been sightings of catfish in the broads. These fish are ferocious predators and could well upset the balance of aquatic wildlife. Casual and thoughtless introductions like this are fraught with unseen dangers and should be avoided at all costs.

FISH

That there are good sized Pike *Esox lucius* within the waters at the Lound Waterworks may be confirmed by any observant naturalist who has rambled close to the waters. A fish resting in the shallow margins may be startled by the approach of a rambler and might be seen speeding away from the margin only to stop a few feet out and then turn to watch any further movement made by the intruder. At times it may be possible to see many small fish literally jump from the water as they attempt to escape the greedy jaws of a prowling pike and the observant watcher may also witness the taking of duckling by this ruthless predator. It approaches from below and rises to snatch the hapless duckling from the surface of the water and swallows up the victim in its capacious jaws. Many ducklings and the young of other water birds fall victim to the pike during spring.

So far as angling records are concerned, some of the biggest Pike known have been taken from the waters of the broads and anglers still come from near and far to fish for this species. The species is to be found in all of the broads, gravel pits and many private lakes and larger ponds.

Also during spring it is often possible to watch fish such as Bream *Abramis brama*, Roach *Rutilus rutilus* and Rudd *Scardinius erythrophthalmus* spawning in the weedy, shallower areas of the water. Though there are not large numbers of Bream in the reservoirs at Lound, Fitton Lake holds massive heads of the species attracting anglers from all over the country. The Bream especially make a great deal of commotion and disturbance to the water as they heave around and at times almost come out of the water as they disperse their spawn amongst the stems of marginal plants. Most gravel pits are usually stocked with this species and there are some quite large numbers to be found in many of the broads.

Perch *Perca fluviatilis* are quite common in all the freshwater areas whereas the Tench *Tinca tinca* prefers shallower, still, or moving waters. They are occasionally found in the broads but are more likely to be found in lakes, ponds and gravel pits. Sometimes referred to as the "doctor fish" early naturalists believed that ailing or wounded fish would rub themselves against the slimy sides of a Tench in order to obtain a cure for their disorder.

Carp are known to be present in the broads but are seldom seen or caught. Early writers on the subject mention good sized specimens but today they are more likely to be encountered in gravel pits where a certain amount of stocking of this species is known to take place. Since they are a favourite quarry of the freshwater angler they provide an attraction to lure them to such venues, but this can hardly be considered to be a natural situation. This species struggles greatly in the broads at times when high tides increase the salinity within these waters.

There are several species of smaller fish to be found in the freshwaters of our area. Crucian Carp *Carassius crassius*, Gudgeon *Gobio gobio*, Dace *Leuciscus leuciscus* and the Eel *Anguilla anguilla*; although their true status is unknown to the authors.

Chapter 7 — Farmland

THE HABITAT

Farmland is probably the most obviously managed habitat dealt with in this book, and for very good reason it is managed for optimum agricultural production rather than for wildlife. Many modern farmers however, are beginning to farm with wildlife and the natural environment in mind, and are working toward sustainable agriculture. Debate will continue for many years on the pros and cons of organic versus non-organic, and of course on the subject of genetic modification; we must ensure that the environment and wildlife are considered as part of the wider issues.

We are all familiar with the ordered structure of a modern farm, often using very large fields, with fewer and fewer hedgerows left to obstruct the progress of ever larger machines. Modern farm buildings are strictly functional and are far less hospitable to the farmyard birds that have relied on them for so long.

Farming habits too have changed over the years, with a move to more autumn sown cereal crops, leaving less fields of stubble to be used by over-wintering birds as a source of food and shelter. Grass is now often cut earlier and fermented as silage as opposed to cutting later and drying as hay.

More efficient drainage and watercourse management have caused the loss of many acres of wet meadows thus depriving those specialist inhabitants of much needed habitat.

Changes are driven by the need for greater production per hectare and per person employed, which in turn means mechanical harvesting requiring more powerful machinery and evenly maturing crops. The final driver is of course good looking, blemish free, even sized consumer produce. In short, the farming industry is driven by the requirements of the consumer, and does its best to preserve the natural environment whilst giving us what we demand; a very difficult balancing act.

PLANTS

Many naturalists believe that farmland with its field edges, and many country lanes and hedgerows, are the most important nature reserves of our area. One of the plants that can be found in these areas is Charlock *Sinapis arvensis* which is probably native. This annual, rough hairy plant which flowers June to August holds its seed pods away from the stem. Formerly of arable land, but now mainly restricted to the hedgerows and waste places by herbicide sprays, it is hated by the farmer as it is one of the most choking plants of the land especially where crops are spring sown.

Common Poppy *Papavar rhoeas* is a species that is found growing with Charlock and other farmland herbs in the hedgerows and wasteland. The once-familiar sight of poppies covering a whole field with a blaze of red is now mostly unseen. However, three to four years ago when a meadow at Burgh Castle was ploughed up, dormant poppy seeds germinated in the disturbed ground and the next year brought a sudden burst of colour. This is also often seen following road works or other ground disturbing activity.

Another plant of our countryside hedgerows is the Bulbous Buttercup *Ranunculus bulbosus*. It is easily recognised as it is normally the first buttercup of the year to bloom. Other identifying features are the sepals which are bent back, the base of the stem is swollen and each leaf has a stalked middle lobe. This Buttercup prefers drier grassland. The name Buttercup dates back to the 18th century. Before that, the flowers were known as butterflower or crowfoot, a name now restricted to white-flowered species growing in ponds, streams and rivers.

The Creeping Buttercup R. repens is also very common on field edges and roadsides. It has a creeping habit, hence its name, and will root at every leaf joint given the opportunity. It can be identified by the pale markings on the leaves.

Another member of the ranunculus family to be found in this habitat is the Lesser Celandine R. ficaria. This can be found in meadows and woodland and is also widely present in the towns and villages.

A very common perennial found on hedge banks and in woods and grassy places, Germander Speedwell Veronica chamaedrys has small blue flowers which, peering out of the foliage on a summers day, remind some people of eyes giving rise to the alternative name of Bird's Eye Speedwell. The speedwells are easily confused one with another, being of similar general appearance.

An annual introduced from Europe in the 19th century, the Common Field Speedwell V. persica was first recorded in Norfolk in 1860 and is now quite common.

Wall Speedwell V. arvensis is one of the small numbers of plants that can grow in the crevices of old walls. Their natural habitat is on dry walls and bare soils, especially heaths, and the flowers are like those of germander speedwell but smaller and almost stalkless. The Ivy-leaved Speedwell V. hederifolia is abundant in arable fields and on grassy verges as well as in woodlands throughout the area.

A common, shade loving, straggly plant of the area, Greater Stitchwort Stelleria holostea needs the support of other plants such as grasses as its stems are very weak. Ancient belief was that because the stems snapped easily they must clearly help to heal broken bones and it is from the Greek words holos and osteon that mean "whole" and "bone" that the botanical name is derived. The short stems of this plant are usually flowerless with only the longer stems bearing the attractive white flowers.

A much rarer, but very beautiful plant, is the Bee Orchid Ophrys apifera. In locations where it is found many plants may be present but it is not widespread. Its name derives from the fact that the lower central petal bears a striking resemblance to a bee both in colour and in size. Early cutting of grassy margins is very damaging to the survival of this species.

Greater Stitchwort

Creeping Thistle Cirsium arvense has a sweet musky odour, which is most attractive to butterflies, and in the summer months many different species can be seen feeding on it. This is our most common thistle and although it normally has pale lilac flowers, they can on occasions be white and have often been recorded as such at Lound Ponds.

An attractive, but very troublesome, weed of farmland the Field Bindweed Convolvulus arvensis has been given the country name of "devils guts" as it wraps itself around other plants and strangles them as they grow. The flower has short, rounded sepals and there are five broad mauve stripes on the underside of the petals. The leaves are alternate up the stems, which twist around and scramble over other plants.

Black Bindweed *Fallopia convolvulus* is a plant of cultivated ground and twines itself amongst the stalks of taller plants. It has black fruits cased in sepals and although its leaves are very similar to those of Field Bindweed it has very different flowers and is not of the same family.

Another common plant of the roadside is the Nipplewort *Lapsana communis*. It is a native plant, which is known to have been growing in Britain since Stone Age times. Its pale yellow flower-heads are rather insignificant, particularly as they are open for only part of the day; it is also common in waste ground, hedges and wood margins.

Field Pennycress *Thlaspi arvense* is a hairy plant with an upright leafy stem, sometimes branched, that lengthens greatly when in fruit. The fruit itself is broadly winged, oval, flattened and notched and when ripe its bright yellow colour makes a conspicuous display in the countryside; it is said to resemble a penny from which the plant derives its name.

A species that is quick to establish itself wherever soil has been disturbed is the Prickly Sow Thistle *Sonchus asper*. This is an upright plant with very few branches and is widespread throughout our area. When cut a white milky fluid or latex is produced, this being the same as that produced by most of the daisy family, including lettuce and chicory.

A common plant of waste ground, the Corn Spurrey *Spergula arvensis*, often invades crops as a troublesome weed. The stems spread at the base but soon bend sharply upwards to grow vertically. Because of its disastrous effect on grain yields it became known as "Pickpurse".

Ground Elder *Aegopodium podagraria* is a troublesome weed of gardens and waste places and near buildings in country villages. The flower head has 10-20 branches and becomes flatter topped when in fruit; the flower has notched petals and prominent stamens, which give a yellowish colour to the flower head.

Sun Spurge *Euphorbia helioscopia* is a common plant of the area and is abundant on cultivated ground. The plant generally has a single stem but can be branched near the base. Bracts below the flowers resemble the oval, stalkless and finely toothed leaves. The plant grows up to 45cm and flowers from April to October.

Petty Spurge *Euphorbia peplus* is a smaller version of the Sun Spurge above. The "flower-head" consists of a number of male flowers, each with a single stamen, surrounding a female flower represented by a stalked ovary.

A very common native plant of dry waste places is Annual Wall Rocket *Diplotaxis muralis*. It has unbranched stems and lobed leaves that form a rosette at the base. If you crush the stem of this plant in your hand the sap will give off a vile hydrogen sulphide smell, hence the alternative name of "stinkweed".

Common Nettle *Urtica dioica* is very widespread throughout the area in all habitats whereas the Small Nettle *U. urens*, which has a milder sting and does not form patches is far less common.

Once believed to be associated with magic, it was known as fairy's wand or fairy's rod in south-western England, Agrimony *Agrimonia eupatoria* is common around the area on field margins, road verges and hedgerows. The stems are upright, unbranched and hairy and it blooms from June to August with numerous starry yellow flowers. A strong yellow dye made from Agrimony was used to colour wool; an alternative common name is Aaron's Rod.

The upright smooth stems of Hemlock *Conium maculatum* are found by roadsides, ponds and waste ground; they are greyish in colour and covered with purple spots. The leaves of the plant are finely divided and it flowers through June and July. This plant is very poisonous.

Honeysuckle *Lonicera periclymenum* is a very common climber of the hedgerows. It bears heads of creamy flowers often laced with red or purple and night flying moths are attracted by its scent, which is strongest at dusk. Its bright scarlet berries add colour to the autumn hedgerow.

A very complex aggregate that is very perplexing to botanists, with around 2,000 varieties and micro-species, is the Bramble *Rubus fruticosus agg*. The flowers can be white or pink and are 20-30mm in diameter in loose panicles. It is very common in this area with many species, with lots having been identified by local specialist Alec Bull. According to old folklore, blackberries, the fruit of the Bramble, should not be eaten after Michaelmas (Sept. 29th) because the devil then spits on them. This advice is quite sound as by then the Flesh Fly is dribbling on them so as to suck up the juice.

Among the many shrubs which grow in our hedgerows is the Blackthorn *Prunus spinosa*. This large shrub, or sometimes small tree, is very common to this area and as well as growing in field hedgerows is found on the edge of small woods and plantations everywhere. It is spread by suckers and can form impenetrable thickets. The white blossom appears in early spring before the leaves and when it does so in March, during cold easterly winds, this period is traditionally known as a "blackthorn winter". Other species of *Prunus* such as the Cherry plum *P. cerasifera* and also sub species of *P. Domestica* are very common in the area but are difficult to define because of hybridisation.

In this area the Field Maple *Acer campestre* is usually seen as a hedgerow shrub growing in mainly chalky soil, and is clipped back to form a neatly trimmed hedge. The leaves are opposite and smallish, with three main round tipped lobes and two smaller basal lobes; in autumn the leaves turn an amber yellow.

Spindle *Euonymus europaeus* occurs only occasionally in this area. For most of the year it is an inconspicuous shrub, but in the autumn it makes itself into a grand sight with its display of dark red leaves and pinkish-red, four-lobed fruits.

Dogwood *Cornus sanguinea* is a deciduous shrub, which is found in the woods and hedgerows of Norfolk on clay soils. It is not common in this area, except where it has been planted, and can be recognised by its red twigs looking very conspicuous in the winter months.

The yellow catkins or "lambstails" of Hazel *Corylus avellana* often provide the only colour in the hedgerows in early spring.

A native of Asia Minor, the Rhododendron *Rhododendron ponticum*, now grows wild in many parts of our area; it is a lover of acid soils. This evergreen shrub, with dark green glossy foliage, can grow to 6m in height spreading rapidly and smothering all other plants in its vicinity. It has been planted locally at such places as Lound, Fritton and Waveney Forest.

Elder *Sambucus nigra* is our only substantial native shrub with compound leaves. It flourishes wherever the nitrogen content of the soil is high, such as abandoned cottages, churchyards and rabbit warrens. It colonises an area quickly and soon becomes established and is the first shrub in the spring to show green leaves.

BIRDS

As one would imagine, arable land dominates much of the area covered by this publication. Sadly, hedgerows formerly associated with farmland areas are now much less a strong feature and many have disappeared altogether. A large percentage of these have gone in recent years as fields have become larger and of the hedgerows that are left, many have been trimmed back to meet agricultural requirements.

Many typical birds of these farmland areas have decreased in numbers which mirrors declines in populations elsewhere in the British Isles. A surprise in recent years however, has been the large numbers of Pink-footed Geese feeding on arable land - mainly on sugar beet tops - between November and early January in areas immediately north and west of Yarmouth. This is a completely new feature due to the Pink-footed Goose populations both increasing and shifting southwards in recent years. After January, these geese will generally move onto grasslands to feed and also to a lesser extent, on winter wheat until departure in mid-March. Several thousand birds are often involved and to see this number feeding in one particular field is a spectacular sight. The only other wildfowl species to regularly frequent arable land is the Mallard where it often feeds in stubble fields in late autumn.

Of the raptors, Sparrowhawks have increased in recent years and can regularly be seen hunting along hedgerows or pursuing small birds over fields. Kestrels are also a feature of open countryside and hovering birds, looking for prey, are frequently seen. Other birds of prey are always possible, but Sparrowhawks and Kestrels are by far the most common.

Game birds are represented by the colourful Pheasant and by both the Red-legged and Grey Partridges whilst Quail can occasionally be encountered in the summer months. The large and very versatile Pheasant is an obvious bird in many areas with large numbers being artificially reared for sporting purposes. In the East Somerton area, white varieties of Pheasant appear with some regularity and small groups are not unknown. Red-legged Partridge numbers have decreased in many areas, but it is still the variety regularly seen as numbers of the Grey Partridge have decreased alarmingly, certainly more so than the former species. This Partridge, often referred to as the English Partridge, is a lover of more grassy areas and it will be interesting to see what effects the new set-aside schemes will have on their numbers. The tiny Quail is strictly a summer visitor and can sometimes be heard calling its characteristic song from stands of wheat or barley; actually seeing one however, is a different matter! The very rare Corncrake, a lover of long lush grass meadows, is now unknown in this area as a breeding species. The last calling birds were recorded at Hemsby in 1931 and in the Ormesby area in 1947. Migrant birds are still possible however, and one was killed on Gorleston seafront in September 1992.

Wading birds are as expected, rare in this habitat but Oystercatchers occasionally breed in arable fields and a few pairs of Lapwings may possibly breed here and there. The latter species was once a very familiar farmland bird in summer, but modern farming methods have changed all that. However, despite the loss in summer, winter flocks have actually increased and Lapwings, and often Golden Plovers, can sometimes be seen in considerable numbers between November and March. Other wading birds may occasionally include Curlew, and Snipe are often attracted to flooded stubble fields.

Large flocks of Black-headed Gulls are often to be found in fields especially when ploughing is in progress. Smaller numbers of Common Gulls are also to be seen with them. Increasingly, groups of the larger gulls, especially Lesser Black-backed and Herring Gulls, are found loafing in large fields near the coast, particularly in late autumn.

The Wood Pigeon is very common everywhere whilst the slightly smaller Stock Dove has a more restricted range. Turtle Doves are summer visitors, in smaller numbers than previously, whilst increasing numbers of Collared Doves are often found in farmlands feeding on spilt grain. The familiar Cuckoo appears in mid to late April and their distinctive calls are eagerly awaited by country folk. However, their stay is often short and many have already departed by late July.

Of the Owls, it is the Barn Owl and the Little Owl which are most likely in farmland areas. Sadly both have decreased in numbers, the former living mostly in old barns and outbuildings and the latter in old roadside trees.

The Skylark is another once familiar farmland species that has shown a definite decrease, both as a breeding species and as a winter visitor. Fields left to stubble over winter, for the increasingly rare spring sown wheat, are particularly favoured by this nondescript species. Around farm buildings, look for Swallows which are present from mid-April to early October whilst House Martins prefer to nest under the eaves of the farms themselves. Other passerines likely to be seen are Meadow Pipit, Pied Wagtail, Wren and Robin. Thrushes such as Blackbirds and Mistle Thrushes haunt hedgerows and in winter are accompanied by flocks of roving Redwings and Fieldfares. Warbler species found in hedgerows include both Whitethroats and Lesser Whitethroats, although many other species of warbler are always possible along with parties of tits of several species.

Carrion Crows and their similar relative, the Rook are both characteristic farmland birds, the latter species' nesting sites often being a feature of a particular village. The distinctive black and white Magpie has increased in all areas and farmland is no exception. Small groups or even flocks are now regularly recorded. The smaller Jackdaw is a resident in lesser numbers and migrants from Scandinavia increase the population in the winter months. The well known Starling has actually decreased in numbers, but this is often hard to believe when great swarms are seen in winter and early spring. Many depart in April to breeding sites on the continent. House Sparrows are also in decline, but this versatile species is still relatively common in some localities unlike the Tree Sparrow, which is now rare.

Large finch flocks were once a very common sight in farmland areas in winter, but are now much less so. Flocks often comprised of Chaffinch, Brambling, Linnet, Greenfinch and Goldfinch; all certainly still occur, but in much reduced numbers. The Yellowhammer with its distinctive and charming song, was once a very common bird of hedgerows and farmland. Its range now is very restricted and much fragmented due to hedgerow loss. Its alarming decrease is much cause for concern. A survey in villages close to Yarmouth in 1960 revealed 160 breeding pairs. A similar survey in 1996 revealed only 19-20 pairs. Likewise, Corn Bunting numbers have declined, perhaps even more dramatically than the Yellowhammer and only a handful of breeding pairs remain. Their jingly song may soon be a thing of the past.

Linnet

MAMMALS

When compared with birds the number of mammals found generally in the countryside is small and this situation applies equally to farmlands. Over the years by far the greatest pest that the farmer has had to cope with around farm buildings has undoubtedly been the Brown Rat *Rattus norvegicus*. Although rats are still a cause for concern to the farmer, they are much less of a problem than in the past, chemical destruction has again played its part in keeping down numbers and consequently the damage caused by this creature has also been reduced considerably. Rats breed at a prolific rate. A female may breed while as young as eight weeks old and produce litters of 6 to 10 young up to six times a year. Mathematics will tell us that with an average of 5 litters per year and 8 young per litter, a single female may produce 40 young per year. If she only lives for two years, the total could be 80 young rats. If half of these youngsters are females they may also begin to breed at eight weeks old and it is therefore not difficult to realise just how their numbers could escalate if no control is exercised.

Another prolific breeder is the Common Rabbit *Oryctolagus cuniculus*. A doe can produce young from the age of six months and having 4 or 5 litters a year with 5 or 6 young to each litter can produce, in theory, as many as 25 youngsters on her own. Needless to say that with such a high reproduction rate, the mortality rate must also be very high from natural causes otherwise the countryside would literally be overrun with rabbits. Stoats are the biggest enemy of the rabbit for they can take and kill rabbits of any size, but the young rabbits fall prey to a greater number of predators. Kestrels have been seen to take the smallest of the rabbits, as have some of the other raptors. Although the usual prey of the Weasel is mice and voles, they have been known to take smaller rabbits at times when the opportunity presents itself. Even the common cat is not ruled out as an occasional predator of the young rabbit, especially around farms.

Myxomatosis has over the years accounted for probably millions of rabbits and although there are still a great many rabbits to be found in and around our recording area, there are always a few that are carrying the disease even today.

The Brown Hare *Lepus capensis*, is found much less frequently today and the sighting of a hare in certain locations is something of a rarity. It was never as abundant as the rabbit and although it does cause some damage to crops and trees, it has never caused the same degree of damage as the rabbit, because of its smaller numbers. Generally on the farm hares are seen singly though on occasions they may be seen in small groups in meadows, arable fields or along hedgerows. Quite often the form, as the home of the hare is known, may be at the base of a hedgerow where they can lie up under a certain degree of cover. They tend to like the open spaces where there is at least some taller growing vegetation that will provide cover when they deem it necessary, and it is not unusual to see them out in the middle of a field. The hare is much larger than the rabbit and has proportionately longer back legs. It is an agile runner and there are not many creatures that can outrun a hare in a straight run. The fox occasionally takes a hare, though more by cunning than by speed. It is said that hares have outstanding vision and upon examination it will be noticed that its eyes are so positioned that it can see sideways and behind. Thus its powers of sight make it extremely difficult for any predator to stalk it from those angles but its forward vision is less acute and it may sometimes fail to see immediate danger right in front of it.

Stoats *Mustela erminea* as previously mentioned feed on rabbits but like weasels will also take smaller rodents; mice, voles and shrews are all included in its diet. Its stealth in hunting is legendary and it will climb trees to take eggs and smaller birds from nests just as easily as it will hunt underground. It is truly a savage predator and its needle-sharp teeth will easily penetrate the toughest skin. The colouration of the stoat is not subject to a great deal of variation other than the fact that it has the ability to turn white during the winter months. Consequently varying degrees of white may therefore be seen in the colouring of its coat as winter approaches, but generally its coat is chestnut brown with creamy white under-parts. It has a black tip to its tail and when the stoat is white, or in ermine as it is called, this can be clearly seen.

The Weasel *Mustela nivalis* is slightly smaller in its build than the stoat but its ferocity, if anything, is greater. For its size it is probably the fiercest fighter in the wild. Although it can, and occasionally does, kill rabbits it is usually smaller ones that are taken. Small birds also form part of its diet, as do all of the smaller rodents. Unlike the Stoat, the Weasel is subject to quite a lot of variation with regard to its colouration. It bears the creamy-white front and under-parts of the stoat but the upper coat is normally sandy brown, although specimens have been seen with much lighter and darker coats or a combination of the two.

Both of these creatures may be considered of some economic importance in that they each tend to control pest species such as rabbits, rats and mice. They are however responsible for some damage to the countryside in that they also take smaller birds and are very fond of eggs.

Many folk who have never seen a live Mole *Talpa europaea* are nevertheless quite aware of its activities and presence, and farmers have little to say in its defence. The mole spends most of its life underground and usually sees little daylight and therefore has little need for good eyesight; all of its activities and hunting are confined to its tunnels. It has an insatiable appetite and cannot live for more than a few hours without food. It feeds mainly on earthworms and consequently it may be said that it deprives the countryside of this useful and valuable ally. On the other hand it devours large numbers of wireworms and other pests of the soil including leatherjackets and therefore its economic importance is very difficult to determine. There is little evidence that it feeds on vegetative matter. Only during prolonged hot and dry summers will the mole venture above ground in search of water, when the ground becomes dry and hard and the food it so desperately needs becomes difficult to find.

Both the Common Field Vole *Microtus agrestis* and the Bank Vole *Clethrionomys glareolus*, are found in our area though becoming less common; they are considered to be pests to agriculture. The common field vole is considered worse because of its propensity for attacking a variety of agricultural produce. It is a prolific seed eater and consequently is an enemy of cereal crops and is also disliked by the farmer because of its habit of digging tunnels just below the surface of the soil, where the roots of crops are growing. The bank vole, as its name implies, is more at home in banks surrounding fields and is much less of a pest to the farmer. Neither of the species are found in large enough numbers to be the cause of too much damage.

Another enemy of the farmer in the past has been the House Mouse *Mus domesticus*, though it has to be said that it is by no means as common today is it once was. The Norfolk Mammal Report for 1996 shows only one record for the species and the same publication for 1997 shows only six records at only five sites for the whole of Norfolk. From this it would appear that the house mouse is a relatively scarce creature and it would be fair to say that if it disappeared altogether not many folk would mourn its demise, perhaps naturalists excepted, for no naturalist is in favour of the extinction of a native species.

The tiny Harvest Mouse *Micromys minutus* is, with the exception of the Pygmy Shrew *Sorex minutus*, the smallest of the British mammals; it weighs less than a quarter of an ounce. It is a very rare and local creature and most of the records received relate only to nests rather than the creature itself. One was found at Lound Waterworks on 11th August 1998, but with only very scarce records it has to be treated as a species in sharp decline and perhaps endangered to some extent.

The Fox *Vulpes vulpes* is probably one of the most beautiful creatures of the British countryside, but its reputation does not match its beauty. It is considered an outlaw in nature for it is extremely cunning and underhand in its ways and the familiar saying "as cunning as a fox" is not an exaggeration by any means. In the wild, rabbits are an important part of the fox's diet but its liking for poultry is the sole cause of the hatred of the farmer and those who specialise in keeping poultry commercially. Rats, small rodents, frogs and some insects are all taken by the fox and if he chances upon a road casualty lying on the highway, he will even attempt to retrieve this, sometimes in broad daylight. There is no doubt that the fox is increasing in numbers especially during the last few years and many motorists report having seen them in their headlights while driving at night.

INSECTS

Most of the insects found in farms and on farmland are not the popular, brightly coloured specimens, but such as weevils, aphids and the larva of many flies and beetles.

Perhaps the best known of crop pests is the dreaded Colorado Beetle *Leptinotarsa decemlieata*; this creature has become notorious as a pest of potatoes in Britain. Originally from the semi-desert areas of Colorado USA it has spread into Europe and subsequently to Britain and many remedial and control methods have had to be adopted to keep the creature under control. The beetle hibernates in the soil and becomes active during May when the females lay hundreds of eggs on the undersides of the leaves. These hatch in a little over a week and the feeding frenzy begins with both larva and the adult beetle feeding on the leaves of potato plants doing great damage to the crop. When the larva are full grown they crawl back to the soil to pupate and within three weeks they emerge as adults, the females of which lay more eggs and the process begins again. It is evident from this that stringent control measures are necessary to keep this pest under control. Any sightings of this creature, larva or adult, must be reported to the police immediately.

Also associated with potatoes is the Death-head Hawk-moth *Acherontia atropus*. This is the largest moth known in Europe and migrates here from Africa. It is not very common but is found occasionally. The females lay their eggs on potatoes and other nightshades and the larva feed on the leaves of the plants. The moth is quite striking and a marking on its thorax is supposed to resemble a skull, giving rise to the creature's name, but it is very variable.

It is well known by most people that the Large White Butterfly *Pieris brassicae* (or cabbage white as it is sometimes called) lays its eggs on brassicas and is therefore responsible for the subsequent damage caused by the caterpillars to such as cabbages and cauliflowers. Those who farm these products commercially have to remain vigilant, for if the caterpillars take a hold the leaves of the plants are rendered useless and what good is a cabbage with no leaves. In addition to the control measures taken by the farmer or gardener, there is fortunately a natural control in the shape of a small and largely insignificant creature known as a Braconid and called *Apanteles glomeratus*. The females are equipped with a long ovipositor (or egg-laying apparatus) which they insert through the skin of the live caterpillar and deposit their eggs into the hapless victim. The eggs hatch inside the caterpillar and begin to eat the flesh of the creature leaving the vital organs to keep the caterpillar alive for as long as possible. Eventually they eat these as well and the caterpillar dies a horrible death. Their dastardly deed done, the maggot-like larva of the parasite crawl from the caterpillar through the pores in the skin and form their cocoons close by and the adults eventually emerge to seek new caterpillars. During years when there are heavy influxes of white butterflies from the continent, these braconids are also greater in numbers thus keeping some control on the caterpillars naturally.

There are a great many insects to be found in the fields of our farmlands and it has to be said that the farmer considers most of them to be pests in one way or another.

There are leather-jackets, larvae of the Crane Flies *Tipula oleracea* and *T. paludosa* and wireworms, larvae of the Click Beetle *Agriotes lineatus* that are soil dwellers and both very damaging to crops.

There are flies such as the Cabbage-root Fly *Delia radicum* whose larva attack the roots of young brassicas, hoverfly larva that feed on bulbous plants and the pea midge that attacks peas. There is much for the farmer to be concerned about when he thinks of insects in his fields.

However, there are many insects such as butterflies and dragonflies that visit his fields and rest on his crops causing no damage at all. They may simply be passing through and attracted to a nectar source, or in the case of dragonflies, the attraction may be the small insects that give rise to the farmer's concern.

Only a few of the insects associated with farmlands have been mentioned here but there are many more not really within the scope of this book. Many require close examination to identify them with a microscope or powerful hand lens being required. This book has dealt with the more easily identified creatures that may be found fairly readily by almost anyone who may take an interest. The more serious student has other options open to him to further his studies. There are many books that he may use that cover the subject in far greater detail.

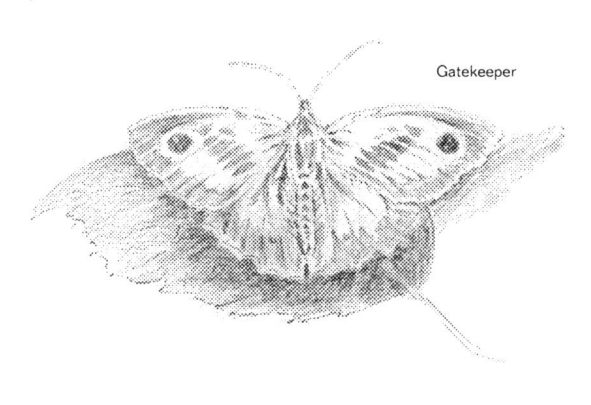

Gatekeeper

Many farms have a pond within their bounds that may have a number of uses. It may provide a drinking point for farm animals, it may provide a source of water during drought conditions, it may serve purely as a drainage pond, or any combination of the three. Whatever its use the farm pond will serve as host to lots of aquatic creatures as well as those that may be passing visitors. These are covered in the chapters on marshland and inland freshwater and so are not dealt with in detail here.

Chapter 8 — Lowland Heath

THE HABITAT

Following the ice age most of lowland Britain became covered by forest. As man's need to grow food crops developed so did his need for land on which to do so. The answer was to create open land from forest and the easiest way to do this was to grub out trees from the lighter soils. Easiest from the point of view of taking out the trees and also from the point of view of subsequently working the exposed land. The exposure of this light land to the elements, particularly the rain, lead to any nutrients in the soil being washed deep, beyond the roots of crops, creating poor quality soils and a need to extend the cleared areas: thus was lowland heath born.

Not a totally natural habitat but, even in those very early days, heavily influenced by man and his needs. This poor quality land was soon invaded by heather and gorse and in an attempt to maintain some level of agricultural activity this vegetation was regularly burned back, introducing some nutrients to the soil but also, encouraging the invasion by bracken. In later years lowland heath was also used for rough grazing which, along with the burning back maintained the heath as open land preventing the regression to woodland.

Heathland which developed in the main from the result of man's interference, became an important wildlife habitat and home to the creatures described in this chapter. Ironically this valuable wildlife resource is itself under threat from the machinations of man as it is once again taken into agriculture, is used as building land by developers or is taken over for leisure purposes such as golf courses. Indeed much of the local heathland has suffered from all three with a major problem being the fragmentation of the area as well as the reduction.

The largest area of lowland heath covered by this book is Belton Common with smaller areas on Fleggburgh Common and some coastal heathland at Winterton. Other tiny fragments remain on Yarmouth North Denes and on Gorleston cliffs towards Hopton. Unless specifically stated the following text refers to Belton Common.

PLANTS

The flora that is found in this habitat includes species such as Bracken *Pteridium aquilinum*, which likes dry acid soils and is often found growing in dense swards. This frost tender plant does well with a little tree cover as is found at Belton Common and the Waveney Forest.

Another plant of acid sandy soils is Sheeps Sorrel *Rumex acetosella*. It can cover large areas and is widespread and common.

Of the grasses to be seen on heathland both Wavy Hair-grass *Deschampsia flexuosa* and Purple Moor-grass *Molinia caerulea* are very common. Wavy Hair-grass is an easy grass to identify. Flowering in June and July, each thin hair-like stalk holds a two-flowered spikelet forming a beautiful sward, especially in bright sunlight, like a mist-covered area of shining silvery reflections. Heathland, and the edge of forest rides, can be carpeted with this species. Purple Moor-grass is a coarse, hairless perennial with wiry stems. Its leaves are stiff, flat and greyish with sheaths of deep purple; it flowers July to September. One other common grass of heathland is Sheep's Fescue *Festuca ovina*. This grass is very common in the area and very variable in appearance. Its hairless and perennial leaves are short, very narrow and inrolled and are almost always a waxy green.

Many of the Cinquefoils *Potentilla* can be rather confusing to a beginner. Of those found on the heathland, Silverweed *P. anserina* is probably the easiest to identify with its unnotched petals and silvery pinnate leaves; it is frequent in this habitat. Tormentil *P. erecta* is widespread and common both on heathland and damp grasslands and Creeping Cinquefoil *P. reptans*, although mainly a grassland plant, is also to be found on Belton Common. There are several others in this family spread over a wide habitat range.

Another pretty little plant to be found in this habitat is Spring Beauty *Claytonia perfoliata*. Its slightly fleshy leaves are in pairs, joining around the stem giving the appearance of the stem growing through the foliage, hence the latin *"per"* through and *"foliata"* foliage. Its tiny flowers have slightly notched petals.

Gorse *Ulex europaeus*, a dense spiny shrub, is common on all remaining pieces of heathland in the area; it grows on well-drained acid soils including coastal cliffs.

Ling *Calluna vulgaris*, also called Heather, is distributed all around the area, the pale purple flowers appearing in August and September.

A native plant of dry grasslands, which is locally common on heathland, is Heath Bedstraw *Galium saxatile*. It is a mat forming perennial with forward facing prickles on the leaf margins. Bird's-foot *Ornithopus perpusillus*, is another native plant of dry sandy and gravelly ground and is found in this habitat especially at Belton Common.

Although our commonest native orchid, the Common Spotted Orchid *Dachtylorhiza fuchsii* is quite rare in our area it is to be found on Belton Common.

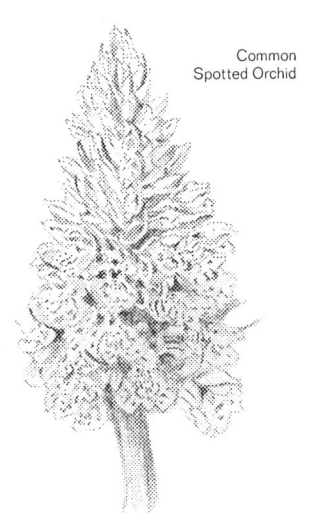

Common Spotted Orchid

TREES AND SHRUBS

Among the trees that are found locally in the heathland habitat are two of the three native species of birch. They are the Silver Birch *Betula pendula* and the White Birch *B. pubescens*. The latter, less common than the Silver Birch, is more tolerant to water and is often to be found in wet hollows; it is also known as the Downy Birch due to the fine hairs on the shoots and leafstalks.

Other trees found on our heaths include Rowan *Sorbus acuparia* and Pedunculate Oak *Quercus robur* but these are mostly planted.

Shrubs such as Hawthorn *Crataegus monogyna* and Bramble *Rubus fruticosus* are also recorded here.

BIRDS

Birds typical of this habitat are Linnets and Yellowhammers, although both have declined in numbers in recent years. Both these species are also typical of farmland areas with hedgerows, but heathland sites are their real home. Stonechats are birds of more coastal heathland areas and a few pairs continue to breed near Winterton and an occasional pair or two have attempted to breed in the Caister Golf course area at Yarmouth North Denes. Formerly, it is on record that Wheatears and Whinchats nested here and obviously were much more widespread in such habitats years ago. Red-backed Shrikes and Nightjars nest in this type of habitat, the latter species still nests close to Winterton Dunes. The Red-backed Shrike ceased to breed locally in the 1970's, although the occasional autumn migrant bird is still seen.

On Belton Common, other species likely to be seen are Blackbird, Song Thrush, Whitethroat, Wren and Dunnock; all these however, are more typical birds of other habitats. The Dartford Warbler is a species which only lives in gorse and heathland habitat and which has expanded its range in recent years from its strongholds in southern England. The first Norfolk record of a Dartford Warbler was one shot at Yarmouth, presumably on the North Denes, in 1846 and a second bird was obtained in February 1859. Recently, a third Dartford Warbler was present for two days in May 1996. It has recently bred in Suffolk making this one species to actively look for in any gorse and heather areas.

MAMMALS

The number of mammals to be found here is not great, a few Grey Squirrels, *Sciurus carolinensis* are occasionally seen in the wooded parts moving around in the tree tops and sometimes on the ground.

Rabbits *Oryctolagus cuniculus* are often seen in the open areas and their droppings are to be seen almost everywhere, indicating that possibly more exist here than may be evident from the sightings.

Mole-hills betray the presence of a few Moles *Talpa europaea* though their numbers do appear to be decreasing in recent years.

The casual walker may at times chance upon a prowling Fox *Vulpes vulpes* or the little Muntjac Deer *Muntjacius reevesi* which seems to be increasing in numbers. Members of the Great Yarmouth Naturalists' Society spotted a Chinese Water Deer *Hydropotes inermis* while on an evening field trip during 1998. Sightings of both Stoats *Mustela erminea* and Weasels *Mustela nivalis* are not uncommon.

INSECTS

1. Butterflies

There are usually around twenty-five species of butterflies to be found on Belton Common and these are normally recorded on an annual basis. During early spring, on warm days, the four species that hibernate during the winter start to make their appearance. The Small Tortoiseshell *Aglais urticae*, Peacock *Inachis io*, Comma *Polygonia c-album* and Brimstone *Gonepteryx rhamni* have each been recorded.

During the last few years there have been occasional sightings of the White Admiral Butterfly *Ladoga camilla* and the Speckled Wood *Pararge aegeria* continues to be recorded regularly; it is felt that this species may be on the increase here.

Along the south-eastern side of the reserve is an old disused railway line. Of course the tracks have all gone and there is little to suggest that a railway ever existed, but there are large spreads of Birds-foot Trefoil *Lotus corniculatus* and Black Medick *Medicago lupulina* to be found growing here as well as on other parts of the heath. These plants provide the preferred food of the caterpillars of the pretty little Common Blue Butterfly *Polyommatus icarus*, sometimes seen in fair numbers.

The Holly Blue *Celastrina argiolus* and the Small Copper *Lycaena phlaeas* have both been recorded and are to be seen regularly. The Purple Hairstreak *Quercusia quercus* may at times be seen around the various oak trees and it may require the observer to search the upper branches with binoculars in order to find it.

The Small Heath *Coenonympha pamphilus* is seen here regularly having, as its name implies, a particular liking for this kind of habitat; it is not commonly seen in many other locations within our area. The Gatekeeper *Pyronia tithonus*, or as it is sometimes called Hedge Brown,

NATURE IN EAST NORFOLK

(49) Common Eider Adult Drake

(50) Grey Hair Grass

(51) Dark-green Fritillary

(52) Seals on Scroby Sands

NATURE IN EAST NORFOLK

(53) Typical Inland Freshwater Habitat - Lound Water

(54) Great Crested Grebe

NATURE IN EAST NORFOLK

(55) Mute Swan and Cygnets

(56) Migrant Hawker

(57) Common Frog

(58) Four-spotted Chaser

(59) Common Mayfly

(60) Unbranched Bur-reed

NATURE IN EAST NORFOLK

(61) Water Dock

(62) Alder Catkins

(63) White Water Lily

NATURE IN EAST NORFOLK

(64) Typical Farmland Habitat

(65) Hawthorn in Flower

(66) Brown Hare

(67) Fieldfare

NATURE IN EAST NORFOLK

(68) Tawny Mining Bee

(69) Bee Orchid

(70) Green-veined White Butterfly

NATURE IN EAST NORFOLK

(71) Typical Heathland Habitat - Belton Common

(72) Silver Birch showing the Witches Broom Gall

(73) Spring Beauty

NATURE IN EAST NORFOLK

(74) Wall Brown Butterfly

(75) Yellowhammer

(76) Grey-dagger Moth

(77) Caterpillar of Grey-dagger Moth

(78) Fly Agaric

(79) Birch Polypore

NATURE IN EAST NORFOLK

(80) Comma

(81) Natterjack Toad

(82) Adder

NATURE IN EAST NORFOLK

(83) Great Grey Slug

(84) Large Black Slug

(85) Garden Snails

(86) Michael Seago

Wall Brown

and the Wall Brown Lasiommata megera, are both quite common, as is the Ringlet Aphantopus hyperantus. Both the Small Skipper Thymelicus sylvestris and the Essex Skipper T. lineola are both to be found here, often in very good numbers.

During 1994 John Burton found the first Brown Argus Butterflies Aricia agestis in this location. In small numbers at first, their numbers have expanded slightly during successive years and they are a regular feature of the heath today.

There is plenty of scope for butterfly enthusiasts here with a very respectable variety of species to study. The food plants of the various butterflies are available and there is ample opportunity for seeking their eggs and caterpillars.

2. Moths

Several of the day-flying moths are to be seen on the common. The red and black coloured Cinnabar Moth Tyria jacobaeae lays its eggs on Ragwort Senecio jacobaea and its many bright orange and black striped caterpillars soon lay waste to the plant.

The Five-spot Burnet Zygaena trifolii has been recorded as has its close relative, the Common Forester Adscita statices which really is a green version of the Burnet: it feeds on Sorrel.

Other day-flying moths recorded are Oak Eggar Lasiocampa quercus, Common Heath Ematurga atomaria, Broad-bordered Bee Hawk-moth Hemaris fuciformis, Vapourer Moth Orgyia antiqua, Muslin Moth Diaphora mendica, Silver Y Moth Autographa gamma, Longhorn Moth Nemophora degeerella, and the micro-moth Adela reaumurella.

The pretty Grey Dagger Moth (Acronicta psi) is a fairly common species. It is nocturnal but during daylight hours is often seen at rest on Birch trunks where it remains fairly well camouflaged.

During an evening walk of the Great Yarmouth Naturalists' Society in 1999, a fine specimen of the Cream-spot Tiger Moth Arctia villica was found; quite a beautiful creature in its own right.

3. Dragonflies

Dragonflies and damselflies are commonly seen on the heath throughout the summer months with the Large Red Damselfly Pyrrhosoma nymphula being the first to appear during late April and followed by the Hairy Hawker Brachytron pratense in early May. Four-spotted Chasers Libellula quadrimaculata and Broad-bodied Chasers Libellula depressa are both to be encountered and are recorded in most years as is the Black-tailed Skimmer Orthetrum cancellatum. The Norfolk Hawker Aeshna isosceles, though more usually found in Broadland, is occasionally seen on the heath, but usually only the odd specimen. The Brown Hawker A. grandis is occasionally seen in fair numbers and sightings of a dozen or more are not uncommon while Southern Hawkers A. cyanea are seen in smaller numbers.

During late summer Migrant Hawkers A. mixta and Common Darters Sympetrum striolatum are often to be seen in large numbers

4. Other Insects

The pine trees bordering the holiday camp to the north attract the largest of our ladybirds, the Eyed Ladybird *Anatis ocellata*. The Cream-streaked Ladybird *Harmonia 4-punctata* and Pine Ladybird *Exochomus 4-pustulatus* are both seen with the latter often over-wintering amongst the gorse bushes on the heath. The Seven-spot *Coccinella 7-punctata*, the Two-spot *Adalia bipunctata*, the Cream-spot *Calvia 14-guttata* and the Fourteen-spot Ladybirds *Propylea 14-punctata* have also been recorded and are commonly seen.

The little Birch Leaf-roller Weevil *Deporaus betulae* is found on the birches and the small red weevil *Attelabus nitens* may be found on young oaks.

Along the sandy footpaths leading to the reserve the Red-banded Sand Wasp *Ammophila sabulosa* may be seen scurrying along the sides of the paths. The antics of this species have been described elsewhere but they are commonly found here.

Another species commonly found here from mid-April to mid-May is the bright and colourful Tawny Mining Bee *Andrena fulva*. Although strictly not a heathland species and perhaps considered a city dweller, it is nevertheless quite common here. It nests in the ground and along the sandy paths, the tiny entrance hole to the nest may be frequently spotted by the more observant.

Hover-Flies are quite numerous on the heath with several species being observed. *Syrphus ribesii*, *Episyrphus balteatus*, *Scaeva pyrastri* and *Volucella pellucens* have all been recorded here, along with the Drone Flies *Eristalis tenax* and *Heliophilus pendula*. Most of the Hover-Flies do not have common names, hence the use of the latin.

Once again there is a great deal of scope and opportunity for studying these colourful creatures for they are regularly seen on the heath and the insect hunter armed with a net may well find species that are new to the heath.

On sunny days the Green Tiger Beetle *Cicindela campestris* may be seen running around on the sandy paths. It can of course fly, but it often chooses to move around on the sand; they do move very fast indeed.

The Great Diving Beetles *Dytiscus marginalis* are often to be seen at the surface of the water in the pond as they take in fresh air supplies. Other aquatic beetles are also to be found within the pond; other regular pond creatures such as Pond-skaters and water boatmen are also seen.

REPTILES AND AMPHIBIANS

On the drier parts of the heath, amongst the heather and bracken, the Adder *Vipera beris* may be seen basking in the early morning sunshine. There are good numbers of this species on the heath. They can be seen lying in small clearings, though close to cover, where they can quickly retreat at any sign of danger. The observer may spot one and the snake, on spotting the observer, will withdraw into the denser vegetation where it will remain for a few minutes. If the observer remains still the snake will no doubt return but any sudden movement will only cause it to retreat again. Obviously the observer should not approach too closely, but with the correct camera and lens, good photographs may be obtained whilst they are basking like this.

Grass Snakes *Natrix natrix* are also found on the heath although with their partiality to damper conditions, most are observed along the edges of the Belton Marshes and the dykes adjacent to the marshes. They can be seen often and regularly.

Slow Worms *Anguis fragilis* and Common Lizards *Lacerta vivipara* are both seen, though it is more a case of being in the right place at the right time. They are slightly more timid than either of the previous species but are still occasionally met with. Many people think that Slow Worms too are snakes, which of course they are not. They are legless lizards and are completely harmless to humans for they feed on slow moving creatures such as slugs and worms.

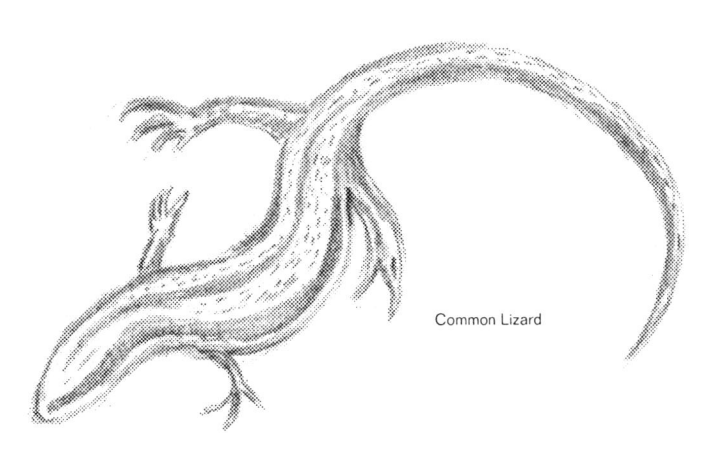

Common Lizard

Some years ago a pond was constructed on Belton Common for the reintroduction of the Natterjack Toad *Bufo calamita* which had previously disappeared from the area. The Natterjack Toad or Running Toad as it is often referred to locally, was regarded as being extremely abundant by A.H.Patterson in 1905, but sadly the reintroduction seems to have been a failure for hardly any specimens have been recorded in the last two or three years.

FUNGI

If the vast numbers of all fungi are considered, then the numbers to be found growing within the heathland habitat is very small indeed; those species to be found in this habitat are those that tend to grow in open drier conditions.

The Fairy-ring Fungus *Marasmius oreades* is generally to be found in any open grassland or meadow but occasionally grows on heaths; it has been recorded at Belton Common on the odd occasion.

Collybia maculata commonly called the Spotted Tough-shank is frequently found growing amongst bracken during late summer and autumn, in clumps or singly. This species is more common in some years than others and may also be found growing in coniferous woodlands.

Mycena sanguinolenta has no common name but may be found growing in heath grassland as well as among lawns in private gardens. It is extremely common but has only appeared at Belton Common spasmodically.

Also without a common name is *M. galopus* and although this species is more usually found growing amongst the leaf litter in woodland, it has been recorded growing along the paths bordering the wooded areas at Belton. *M. filopes* has occasionally been found growing on buried twigs and branches close by the wooded areas. It is very common but cannot be considered a heathland species.

The weird Shaggy Ink Cap *Coprinus commatus* may be found growing on the heath and also in meadows or on wasteland, especially where ground has been disturbed. On maturity the

Shaggy Ink Cap

edges of the cap begin to drip a black inky liquid and they start to dissolve until there is nothing left.

The Common Funnel Cap *Clitocybe infundibuliformis* is so named because of the shape of the cap. It is a very common species and may be found in deciduous woodland within our area and it has also been recorded on Belton Common quite frequently. This species may be found growing during the summer months though is not often seen later than the end of September. It has also been found growing in the more open areas of the Waveney Forest at Fritton.

The Deceiver, *Laccaria laccata* is an extremely common species and may be found in a variety of habitats. It has been recorded regularly on Belton Common as well as Lound Waterworks, usually growing in troops but has been recorded at Lound growing in a circle resembling a fairy ring. It has been found growing prolifically in the heathy areas of the Waveney Forest as well as in the wooded parts.

The species known as the Liberty Cap, *Psilocybe semilanceata* is occasionally found growing here at Belton Common. It is not very common but in years when it is found it may be quite abundant.

There are one or two puffballs that are associated with heaths but within our area only two species have been recorded at Belton Common. *Lycoperdon echinatum*, which may be found growing during the summer until well into autumn and *L. foetidum*, found during the same period. Their spores are spread by the action of raindrops falling on them, which cause the powder-like spores to 'puff' out like fine dust into the atmosphere to be carried farther afield by light breezes. Neither are very common and records for both species are rather spasmodic. They are fairly easily identified in the field being somewhat darker in appearance than most other puffballs.

Chapter 9 — A Miscellany of Nature

This chapter covers some very specialist records such as marine and fresh water molluscs as well as some really unusual and unexpected sightings; a true miscellany. As such it does not follow the set pattern of the previous chapters but will nevertheless provide some interesting reading.

BIRD ESCAPES

With the increasing number of wildlife parks, waterfowl collections and aviaries in the area, it is not surprising that escaped birds occur in the wild much more frequently than before. The variety is quite considerable and in recent years several White Pelicans, Demoiselle Cranes and Chilean, Greater and Caribbean Flamingos have been seen in the Breydon area. Two exotic Crowned Cranes and an African Spoonbill were Gorleston's specialities in 1968 and 1969 respectively.

Waterfowl provide the bulk of the escapes and the lengthy list includes Maned Duck, Silver Teal, Mottled Teal, Cinnamon Teal and Chloe Wigeon.

More interesting was a Red-tailed Hawk that frequented parts of Fritton Decoy in March 1998.

Three Red-headed Buntings seen in the area since 1960 were presumed escapes but, as all three were seen during the late spring period, the possibility of a genuine vagrancy cannot be excluded.

Several varieties of Weaver Birds are kept in captivity and the successful breeding of a pair of Black-headed Weavers in the grounds of Caister Castle in 1989 was very noteworthy; the first time this species had bred in the wild in this country. The long, hot and dry summer of 1989 was doubtless a great advantage to this African species.

Other passerine escapes seen locally include the Peach-faced Lovebird, Sudanese Golden Sparrow, several types of Waxbills and various Parrots, Cockatiels and Zebra Finches.

INSECTS

Many large supermarkets have sprung up in and around the town and the villages in recent years and have now become the accepted way of shopping. On occasions, telephone calls have been received from one or other of the superstores asking for help in regard to unusual creatures discovered among the fruit delivered to them, particularly among bananas. Several Australian Cockroaches *Periplaneta australasiae* and American Cockroaches *P. Americana* have been presented for identification as well as one or two more exotic specimens of the cockroach family. Occasionally they are found alive but they would not usually be able to withstand our winters although with the threats of global warming, who knows what the future may hold in this respect.

Bananas, while still growing on the trees, provide a useful resting place or hideout for lots of smaller creatures and when they are harvested some of the creatures remain within the hands of bananas and are transported with them. Obviously many die during transportation but occasionally some survive and when the bananas are brought into the shops the warmth within the store brings them out and they are then discovered usually causing some alarm to the finder. Sadly most of those who discover such creatures react too quickly with the foot, leaving them beyond identification. Although such creatures are not native here they do provide some interest to the naturalist, especially those involved in the study of entomology.

A Praying Mantis *Mantis religiosa* was found, having arrived in Brazilian melons. This caused some concern to its finder who promptly put his foot on the creature. When brought along for identification it was somewhat squashed and required some delicate work to restore it to some semblance of its original state. It was a simple enough matter to identify the creature but these insects are normally found in Europe and Brazil is not a native home to them. How was it that it arrived in Brazilian melons? Some research was necessary in order to solve the problem. Mantids feed on certain insects and serve a most useful purpose in curtailing the numbers of those creatures. When it was discovered in Brazil that these insects were increasing rapidly in numbers, the Praying Mantis was introduced from Europe in order to attempt to reduce the numbers of these harmful insects. Obviously conditions in Brazil must have been satisfactory to the mantis for it has increased in numbers and has served the purpose intended.

SPIDERS

Spiders are generally quite common although certain species may be very localised with some being quite scarce and others being extremely rare. Unfortunately not very many species of spiders have acquired common names and this sometimes makes it difficult to relate the species to the reader. Most people may know the Garden spider by its common name but if recorded by its scientific name, the species may not be so readily recognised. Therefore the species listed below are those that most folk could easily find either in the garden, around the house, or in the countryside. Species that are difficult to identify or require careful examination under the microscope have been avoided bearing in mind that the purpose of this volume is to guide the reader toward the more commonly found and easily identified creatures.

The Garden Spider *Araneus diadematus* is extremely common in most gardens as well as woods and other suitable habitats and is very attractive in its colouration. It may be found from the late summer and occasionally well into autumn.

Another species from the same family is *A. quadratus* which has been recorded at Lound Waterworks, Belton Common, the Winterton Dunes area and from the north side of Breydon Water. It has a very rounded body ranges between green and red in colour with four pale round spots.

Tegenaria domestica is often called the House Spider for that is where it is usually found. It will occupy out of the way and neglected areas in the house but will occasionally venture out to be seen while the occupants are watching television and all too often it is quickly despatched. There are one or two other species within the genus that may be found in houses but *T. domestica* seems to be the most common.

There is a colourful spider that may well be found around the garden, its carapace is usually reddish brown and the abdomen is buff to pinkish brown: a quite distinctive creature with no common name. Its Latin name is *Dysdera crocata* but it has been called the biting spider, for it will bite in some circumstances and can produce quite a nip. It is a fairly widespread species and has been recorded on the north Breydon wall as well as several other locations.

Another species that to some extent resembles the previous one in appearance is *Drassodes lapidosus* and like it, is found under stones or logs. It has been recorded at Lound Waterworks, Belton Common, Waveney Forest and along the Breydon north wall. It is a fairly common and widespread species.

Those who like to frequent some of the damper areas where reeds, sedges and grasses are to be found growing, may well have noticed that there is a spider that is associated with such habitats. The spider in question is known as *Tibellus oblongus*, and the second part of its Latin name may give a clue to its identity. When seen resting on the narrow leaves of reeds or other grasses with its legs stretched out forwards and behind, it gives the appearance of being oblong in shape. Its body is quite long when compared with other species but perfectly suited for its way of life.

Another spider of a different genus behaves in a similar manner, and in general shape resembles *T. oblongus*. Known as *Tetragantha extensa*, like the previous species, it has a preference for damp places. Both species have been found at Lound waterworks, Blocka Lane, Greens Pits at Burgh Castle and around several marsh dykes within the area.

Many people are surprised to find that there is a spider that spends most of its time underwater. Commonly called the Water Spider it is called *Argyroneta aquatica* and its habits can only really be studied when kept in an aquarium stocked with aquatic plants. The creature constructs a bell shaped structure under water among vegetation that it fills with air bubbles giving it the appearance of a silver globe in the water. It renews the air supply by rising to the surface of the water and taking in fresh air and carrying it down to the nest which may gradually increase in size. During the daytime the spider rests in the bubble but at night it ventures out and hunts in the water for food, which consists of small insects found living in the water; it is strange to watch the creature as it glides in and out of the bubble at will. It has been recorded from many marsh dykes within the area, a small dyke in Lound Waterworks and in the Damgate area at Acle. Some of the dykes on the Haddiscoe marshes produce good numbers of this species and specimens of all sizes may be found while dipping with a net. This seems to be rather a local hotspot.

PLANT GALLS

Despite the fact that there are numerous plant galls to be found throughout the county there are still those who are not aware of their existence. Galls are found on almost all plants and trees and can thus be found in many habitats. They are not always readily visible and, even when they appear on cultivated garden plants, are often overlooked by gardeners.

Galls come in all shapes and sizes and are caused by a variety of sources. Tiny mites are responsible for probably the greatest number including many of the more common species. Others are caused by gall wasps, fungi, bacteria, bugs, beetles and moths and each individual type of gall is identifiable from its general appearance. Of course some are similar in appearance just to make identification that little bit more difficult but the would-be student of "Cecidology" (The study of galls) should therefore examine all plants in order to find peculiarities on the leaves, stems, buds and flowers and catkins where trees are concerned.

The fact that there are so many varieties of galls to be found makes it beyond the scope of this book to attempt to name them all. The aim of the book is to gently prompt readers to seek and enjoy the wonders of nature and not to baffle them with species that require microscopic study for identification.

Thus only a short list of the more commonly found galls have been included to help the reader to recognise them with the aid of a modest field guide.

Galls are produced by the plants or trees themselves and not by any creature. Generally the creature pierces the tissue of the host plant while in the process of laying eggs. The eggs are inserted into the host often together with enzymes, which agitate the plant to produce the malformed vegetation we know as galls.

Perhaps the best known of all the galls is the Oak Apple; not an apple at all but a spongy woody growth found on oak trees during June and July. Caused by the gall-wasp *Biorhiza pallida*, they contain tiny chambers where the larvae develop and whence they emerge. The newly emerged females then penetrate the soil in order to lay their eggs on the fine root hairs of the tree and thus cause another type of gall on the roots known as root galls. Quite often the old oak apples remain on the tree throughout the winter.

Another gall that is easily recognised is the Knopper gall found growing on acorns during the summer. They are often seen almost as soon as the acorns are formed and are caused by the gall-wasp *Andricus quercuscalicis*. In some years they are extremely common with hardly an oak tree that does not have its proliferation of knoppers.

The so-called Artichoke gall is also to be found growing on oak trees. It is caused by a gall-wasp known as *Andricus fecundator*. Two or three galls may be seen growing together on small stalks and as the name implies, resemble artichokes.

Artichoke Gall

Careful examination of the underside of oak leaves will often reveal numerous flat disk shaped growths, sometimes dozens on each leaf. They are caused by the gall-wasp *Neuroterus quercusbaccarum* and are known as common spangle galls. They remain on the leaf throughout the summer and are mature by September when they become detached from the leaf and fall to the ground where they remain, with the larva continuing to develop inside the disc. During April of the following year, females emerge to lay eggs on the oak catkins that later cause the development of the well known currant galls. There are two other spangle galls to be found on oak leaves, the smooth spangle gall caused by the gall-wasp *N. albipes* and the silk button spangle galls caused by the gall-wasp *N. numismalis*.

The Rose Bedeguar gall or perhaps better known as Robin's pin-cushion is to be found growing on wild roses. It is caused by the gall-wasp *Diplolepis rosae* and is probably the most beautiful of all the galls. It usually appears between May and June and will remain on the plant until well into autumn when it blackens, but the larva remain inside and emerge as adults in May. There may be as many as fifty or sixty internal chambers within the gall, which consists of lots of tangled branching filaments, greenish at first then becoming bright red with orange and yellow filaments also intertwined.

The gall-mite *Eriophyes macrorhynchus* is responsible for causing small reddish spikes on the upper surface of the leaves of Sycamore. They appear almost as soon as the leaves are formed and in some years they are extremely prolific with hardly a leaf escaping the attentions of this tiny mite. There may be several hundreds of these galls on each single leaf.

Even the Holly tree does not escape the attentions of a gall causer. The glossy green leaves are often seen bearing a yellowish or reddish blotch attached to the central rib of the leaf. This is caused by the tiny fly *Phytomyza ilicis* whose minute larva is actually a leaf miner. The gall develops during early spring and the fly leaves the leaf during mid to late summer. Careful examination of the leaf at the end of summer will reveal the presence of an exit hole from which the adult fly emerged. A fully grown holly may have several hundreds of its leaves affected by this gall.

Willow leaves may be affected by several galls, some which leave additional growths on their leaves, some which leave the leaf slightly distorted and some which twist the leaves completely out of shape. The Bean gall appears in a yellow and a red stage and leaves a bean-shaped growth within the structure of the leaf. It is caused by the Sawfly *Pontania proxima*, which produces two broods each year. The first brood, the result of eggs having been laid in the leaf bud during May, is full grown by June and July, while the second brood, from eggs laid in August, reaches a similar stage in September and October. These grubs gradually devour the cavity of the gall and when fully fed, leave the gall and pupate in the ground in a cocoon from which they eventually emerge as adults. The gall-mite known as *Eriophyes marginatus* affects only the margins of the leaves which are caused to curl upwards onto the top of the leaf. These curls contain hundreds of tiny fine hairs among which the mites dwell and remain fairly well concealed. They are first to be found in June and reach maturity during August and September.

By far the largest gall is the unwieldy growth known as the Witches-broom, more often found on Birch but occasionally found on Hazel and Hornbeam. They look like twiggy balls and can appear on almost any part of the stem or the branches and a single tree may carry several; the fungus *Taphrina carpini* causes these galls.

Not only do many of the galls produce a mature creature that has legitimately emerged from the growth but there are many parasites that attack the legal occupant during its various stages. The young of the parasite will usually devour the host and emerge itself as an adult. A fungus, which causes them to fail, occasionally attacks some galls and many must obviously fail for a variety of other reasons.

There are few plants that are not utilised as gall carriers and the interested observer may derive much pleasure in his search for the variety of species. Sadly he is not aided by an abundance of literature on the subject although new literature does appear from time to time. However, this should not be off-putting to the student for there is enormous interest and enjoyment to be gained and there is still much new ground to cover and new finds are regularly being made.

FRESHWATER MOLLUSCS

There are both land molluscs and those that spend the greater part of their lives in water, some occasionally rising above the surface of the water on the stems of emergent plants, though they are really creatures of the water. There are also molluscs to be found in saline or brackish waters.

Some species are known by common names whereas some are only known by their scientific Latin names. A certain amount of survey work has been carried out on the Lound Waterworks reserve during the past few years and many of the following records have been compiled by Dr. Roy Baker, Keith Clarke and Derek Howlett. The authors are extremely grateful for their contribution to this otherwise 'little recorded' group. Records of marine species are the result of a survey of Breydon Water.

The smallish White Ramshorn Snail *Gyraulus albus* is frequently found at Lound and the Whirlpool Ramshorn Snail *Anisus vortex* is common in many Norfolk waters. These species are generally recognisable by their flat coiled appearance as is the much larger Great Ramshorn Snail *Planorbarius corneus*. The Great Ramshorn Snail is quite an interesting creature to observe when kept in a freshwater aquarium.

The Jenkins' Spire Shell *Potamopyrgus jenkins* is very common at Lound and may also be found in other freshwaters whereas the Ear Pond Snail *Lymnaea auricularia* is only occasionally found.

Some of the larger species to be found in freshwaters are quite impressive looking creatures such as the Swan Mussel *Anodonta cygnea*. There is a very healthy population at

Lound mainly near the margins of the ponds rather than in the deeper, peaty bottomed areas. The slightly similar Duck Mussel *Anodonta anatine* is perhaps less common than the previous species but nevertheless fairly common. The Painters Mussel *Nio pictorum* is occasionally found near the margins at Lound.

There are several other species occuring at Lound but they have no common name and are beyond the scope of this book.

MARINE MOLLUSCS

The Sand Gaper *Mya arenaria* is widely distributed along the coast. It is to be found in sand, mud and sand-mud areas in the lower sections of estuaries and can live to depths of 73 metres.

The Common Mussel *Mytilis edulis* used to be extremely common beneath the old wooden Dutch pier at Gorleston but since the building of the piled and concrete structure they no longer exist there. Only odd speciemens are found near Breydon Bridge near the seaward end of Breydon Water.

The Rough Periwinkle *Littorina saxatilis* is a viviparous species and is commonly found on stony and rocky beaches in the barnacle zone. The rocky sea defences that line the banks of Breydon Water provide excellent conditions and are a good habitat for this species.

Another species commonly found in estuaries is the Laver Spire Shell *Hydrobia ulvae*. This species can live permanently in salinities ranging from 5%-33%. It feeds on surface vegetation, mainly diatoms, and silts containing high organic matter. Water movement is an important factor in its distribution hence its regular presence in estuaries. It has been assessed as "numerous and common" in Breydon.

The much favoured and edible Winkle *Littorina littorea* is occasionally found on the salt marshes and mud flats and the Cockle *Ceratoderma glaucum* frequently occurs.

LAND MOLLUSCS

The Common Garden Snail *Helix aspersa* must be instantly recognised by almost everyone. It is commonly found in gardens and almost any waste grassland often in quite large numbers. During the winter they may be found under logs or large stones.

The Brown-lipped Snail *Cepaea nemoralis* sometimes called the Grove Snail is extremely common everywhere. It has been recorded on the Bure marshes and Winerton Dunes as well as many of the Waveney marshes, Belton Common, Lound Waterworks and many other locations.

The Amber Snail *Succinea putris* lives in marshes and damper locations and is extremely common and widespread. It is quite variable in shell colouration and ranges from almost deep yellow to the darkest brown.

The Rounded Snail *Discus rotundatus* is also a very common species and can be found among dead leaves and rotten wood.

A few species are known as glass snails due to their slightly transparent shells. Probably the most common locally is the Pellucid Glass Snail *Vitrina pellucida*. It is found under leaves and logs in damp woods. It feeds on earthworms.

The Large Black Slug *Arion ater* is often seen in grasslands in the early morning dew and after a shower of rain. They simply love wet grass. They are instantly recognisable their common name describing them perfectly. Another large species is the Great Grey Slug

Limax maximus, which when fully stretched out may be as long as 80mm. They may be found in gardens and parks under logs and stones and are really quite common. The Yellow Slug *Limax flavus* is a medium sized species occasionally found in gardens and occasionally in woods where it feeds on various species of fungus including the deadly Death Cap *Amanita phalloides* and comes to no harm in digesting the highly poisonous toxins in that species of fungi. The Tree Slug *Lehmannia marginata* as its common name suggests is found on the trunks of trees working its way in and out of the fissures of the bark. It is fairly common in woods and prefers damp weather. It feeds on fungi and lichens on the bark.

There are numerous other species many with no common names. The few species mentioned above are included to whet the appetite of the would be mollusc hunter. There is a great deal of scope for further studies into this most fascinating group.

ARTIFICIAL HABITATS

Most people, with very little outlay and expertise, can create several kinds of artificial mini-habitats. The fascination of keeping all kinds of creatures in confinement in order to study their habits and life styles probably really began in Victorian times; many eminent naturalists of the day had large houses in which to indulge themselves in such a hobby. Much can be learned when creatures are observed every day in a mini- habitat, similar to that in which they would normally be found. Records can be kept daily and many useful observations can be made without having to make daily treks into the wild. Here are one or two suggestions that may inspire the reader to indulge in a closer study into the ways of the creatures of the wild, with little effort on the part of the observer.

An aquarium is not an expensive item these days in fact the handyman can even construct one for himself. This would provide the opportunity to construct a custom made aquarium to suit the purpose required. For the beginner and not so handy nature lover, a bought one will suffice. A tank around 60cm long, 30cm wide and 30cm wide is ideal for the purpose and will hold a good variety of creatures. Pond creatures can be carefully watched in such a tank and this can be a fascinating pastime. Small stones can be purchased from a pet shop and placed in the bottom around 50mm deep in which to anchor plants. The plants may be purchased from any aquarist stores and should be planted thickly to provide good cover for the various aquatic creatures. A book on pond creatures that will explain what these creatures feed on and their habits can be obtained from the local library or purchased from a bookshop; it is of little value to stock the aquarium with creatures that eat each other, as the tank will soon be depleted. Students should determine what it is they wish to study and then satisfy themselves as to where it can be found and set about collecting it. The relevant law with regard to trespass or removing without permission must of course be considered but often the owners of countryside ponds will oblige in this respect. Keeping these aquatic creatures in an aquarium will enable a detailed study to be made, which in the wild would be virtually impossible.

A seed propagator consisting of a seed tray with a high perspex removable lid is ideal for the rearing of caterpillars and moth or butterfly pupae. With regard to rearing pupae, if the tray is filled with peat and the pupae are gently pushed into it they will usually be fairly easy to rear. Of course some species are extremely difficult but most of the common species will rear easily enough. It is necessary to keep the container in a cool place for if kept in the warmth of a centrally heated house the adults will emerge too soon and there will be no available food on which to feed them. Usually pupae in the wild are buried in the ground or under bark or some other material and are able to withstand quite low temperatures and consequently will come to little harm. The process is extremely fascinating especially if the student is on hand when the moth or butterfly actually emerges.

So far as the rearing of caterpillars is concerned, it is necessary to first ascertain what the caterpillar actually feeds on and to then obtain a good supply of this. Depending on the number of caterpillars being reared, sufficient food should be placed in the container and sprayed regularly with water in order to keep it as fresh as possible for they will otherwise soon die; replacing the food on a regular basis is often necessary. When the caterpillar is fully fed it will usually change colour and then empty itself of bodily waste and begin to form its cocoon or pupa depending on the species and will then begin its metamorphosis. Again depending on the species being reared it will spend a certain amount of time in this way before emerging as the adult insect. Once again it is truly fascinating to rear these creatures and a great deal can be learned of their ways by anyone with an interest.

In order to study ants an earth filled glass container, such as a small aquarium, is ideal providing it is partitioned off to create a very narrow space. This ensures that some runs will be made up against the glass enabling them to be observed quite easily. The same applies to the study of earthworms when a container probably 30cm high by 60cm wide and 5cm deep from front to back will keep the worms close to the front of the container and thus affording a close observation area.

A greenhouse can of course provide the necessary habitat for a butterfly farm. By careful selection the various food-plants for the caterpillars and nectar providing plants for the adults can be planted and caterpillars introduced. Of course all the vents should be covered with very fine gauze in order to retain the occupants and still afford plenty of necessary ventilation. All of the occupants will be confined and thus protected from the usual predators and a good variety of butterflies can be farmed in this way; when the adult butterflies emerge they can be released into the wild.

There are many ways in which the interested and enthusiastic nature lover can gain enjoyment from the hobby and increase his or her knowledge of whatever aspect of natural history takes the fancy. Naturally laws should be obeyed in all respects when taking creatures from the wild and rare or endangered species should not be taken. Only the common species should be considered and after study should be returned to the wild into the location from which they were taken. If these rules are adhered to then the student should be able to learn much about nature without doing any harm to the environment and its inhabitants.

SOME ALIEN PLANTS

In 1696 a former Duke of Argyll, who had ordered some tea plants, was sent in error *Lycium halimifolium* and so the Duke of Argyll's Tea-plant, as it became known, was introduced to the British Isles from the near east. This plant, now called *L. barbarum*, has been introduced to this area and is very common locally in hedgerows.

Another introduction, this time from America where it is a common and troublesome weed is the Thorn Apple *Datura stramonium*. This is a poisonous annual growing up to 36in. (100 cm) high which was grown in the past for its medicinal properties. The leaves are glossy, toothed and spiky and it has trumpet shaped flowers that appear in late summer that can be purple or white. They develop into green thorn apples, a prickly fruit about the size of a Horse Chestnut case. When ripe these fruits split into four from the top, releasing dark kidney shaped seeds which contain atropine, hyoscyamine, and hyoscine which act on the nervous system, causing hallucinations and dilating the pupils of the eyes This is a very sporadic plant of the area found mainly on arable land.

An erect or spreading tuberous perennial from Europe, the Yellow Corydalis *Pseudofumaria lutea* has fern like leaves and dense clusters of golden-yellow spurred flowers. The glossy black seeds are too heavy to be carried by the wind, yet many plants are found on walls and on the side of buildings. This is probably because the seed is oily and fleshy and with the edible parts being attractive to ants, they would be carried off to their nests above or below ground level. Yellow Corydalis is becoming very common especially in the Yarmouth and Gorleston area, and can be found growing on walls and in waste places and can make a very attractive addition to the garden.

The Japanese Knotweed *Fallopia japonica* is a most aggressive and conspicuous plant. It was introduced from Japan in 1825, and was widely grown in 19th century gardens. It now forms dense thickets everywhere it is allowed to grow, invading waste ground, derelict land, railway embankments and cuttings, road verges and the banks of rivers and streams. It is perhaps the worst weed ever to have reached these islands, where its continued and rapid spread includes parts of this area; in many places it is common. The flowering time is from late August to October. The Wildlife and Countryside Act 1981 forbids its introduction into the wild in Britain.

Part 3
An Alphabetical Index of The Flora and Fauna and The Habitats in which they may be found

1. Woodland
2. Marshland
3. Estuary
4. Towns and Villages
5. Coast and Seashore
6. Inland Freshwater
7. Farmland
8. Heathland

SPECIES LIST	\multicolumn{8}{c}{HABITATS}
1. Plants	1	2	3	4	5	6	7	8
Alder Buckthorn (Frangula alnus)	●			●		●		
Alexanders (Smyrnium olusatrum)					●		●	
Annual Meadow Grass (Poa annua)	●	●	●	●	●	●	●	●
Annual Mercury (Mercurialis annua)				●	●	●	●	●
Arrowhead (Sagittaria sagittifolia)		●						
Bee Orchid (Ophrys apifera)							●	
Birdsfoot Trefoil (Lotus corniculatus)		●		●	●		●	●
Bird's-foot (Ornithopus perpusillus)								●
Biting Stonecrop (Sedum acre)				●	●		●	●
Bittersweet (Solanum dulcamara)		●		●	●			●
Black Meddick (Medicago lupulina)		●					●	
Bluebell (Hyacinthoides non-scripta)	●			●	●		●	
Bogbean (Menyanthes trifoliata)		●				●		
Bracken (Pteridium aquilinum)								●
Branched Bur Reed (Sparganium erectum)		●				●		
Broad-leaved Willowherb (Epilobium montanum)				●			●	●
Brooklime (Veronica beccabunga)		●				●		
Bulbous Buttercup (Ranunculus bulbosus)		●		●			●	
Bulrush (Typha latifolia)		●						
Butterfly Bush (Buddleja davidii)				●	●			
Canadian Fleabane (Conyza canadensis)				●	●	●	●	●
Cock's Foot (Dactylis glomerata)	●	●	●	●	●	●	●	●
Common Bent (Agrostis capillaris)	●	●	●	●	●	●	●	●
Common Cleavers (Galium aparine)	●	●		●	●		●	●
Common Dog Violet (Viola riviniana)	●							
Common Duckweed (Lemna minor)		●				●		
Common Fleabane (Pulicaria dysenterica)	●	●						

1. Woodland
2. Marshland
3. Estuary
4. Towns and Villages
5. Coast and Seashore
6. Inland Freshwater
7. Farmland
8. Heathland

SPECIES LIST	HABITATS							
1. Plants (continued)	1	2	3	4	5	6	7	8
Common Ragwort *(Senecio jacobaea)*		•		•	•		•	•
Common Reed *(Phragmites australis)*		•				•		
Common Restharrow *(Ononis repens)*					•		•	•
Common Scurvy Grass *(Cochlearia officinalis)*			•				•	
Common Sedge *(Carex nigra)*		•				•		
Common Sorrel *(Rumex acetosa)*				•	•		•	•
Common Spotted Orchid *(Dactylorhiza fuchsii)*							•	•
Common Twayblade *(Listera ovata)*				•		•		
Common Valerian *(Valeriana officinalis)*		•		•		•		
Confused Michaelmas Daisy *(Aster novi-belgii)*			•					
Creeping Buttercup *(Ranunculus repens)*	•	•		•	•	•	•	•
Creeping Cinquefoil *(Potentilla reptans)*		•				•		•
Cuckooflower *(Cardamine pratensis)*		•				•		
Curled Dock *(Rumex crispus)*	•				•		•	•
Divided Sedge *(Carex divisa)*		•						
Dog's Mercury *(Mercurialis perennis)*	•						•	
Early-purple Orchid *(Orchis mascula)*		•		•				
Eel Grass *(Zostera marina)*			•					
Enchanters Nightshade *(Circaea lutetiana)*	•			•				
False Fox Sedge *(Carex otrubae)*		•						
Fat Duckweed *(Lemna gibba)*		•				•		
Fen Bedstraw *(Galium uliginosum)*		•						
Feverfew *(Tanacetum parthenium)*		•		•	•		•	•
Fools Watercress *(Apium nodiflorum)*		•				•		
Frogbit *(Hydrocharis morsus-ranae)*		•				•		
Garlic Mustard *(Alliaria petiolata)*	•						•	
Gorse *(Ulex europaeus)*					•			•
Great Fen-sedge *(Cladium mariscus)*		•				•		
Greater Pond Sedge *(Carex riparia)*		•				•		
Greater Willowherb *(Epilobium hirsutum)*	•	•		•			•	•
Green-winged Orchid *(Orchis Morio)*					•			
Grey Hair-grass *(Corynephorus canescens)*					•			
Groundsel *(Senecio vulgaris)*				•	•		•	•

PART 3   ALPHABETICAL INDEX OF SPECIES AND THEIR HABITATS   93

1. Woodland
2. Marshland
3. Estuary
4. Towns and Villages
5. Coast and Seashore
6. Inland Freshwater
7. Farmland
8. Heathland

SPECIES LIST	HABITATS							
1. Plants (continued)	1	2	3	4	5	6	7	8
Hare's-foot Clover *(Trifolium arvense)*		●			●			
Heath Bedstraw *(Galium saxatile)*								●
Heather (Ling) *(Calluna vulgaris)*								●
Hemp Agrimony *(Eupatorium cannabinum)*		●				●		
Ivy-leaved Duckweed *(Lemna trisulca)*		●				●		
Ivy-leaved Toadflax *(Cymbalaria muralis)*				●				
Lady's Bedstraw *(Galium verum)*		●				●		
Larkspur *(Consolida ajacis)*				●	●			
Least Duckweed *(Lemna minuta)*		●				●		
Lesser Celandine *(Ranunculus ficaria)*	●			●			●	
Lesser Meadow-rue *(Thalictrum minus)*					●			
Lesser Pond Sedge *(Carex acutiformis)*		●						
Marram *(Ammophila arenaria)*					●			
Marsh Bedstraw *(Galium palustre)*		●						
Marsh Foxtail *(Alopecurus geniculatus)*		●						
Marsh Marigold *(Caltha palustris)*		●				●		
Marsh Pennywort *(Hydrocotyle vulgaris)*		●				●		
Marsh Sow Thistle *(Sonchus palustris)*		●						
Marsh Thistle *(Cirsium palustre)*		●						
Meadow Foxtail *(Alopecurus pratensis)*	●	●	●	●	●	●	●	●
Milk Parsley *(Peucedanum palustre)*		●				●		
Nodding Bur Marigold *(Bidens cernua)*		●						
Ox-eye Daisy *(Leucanthemum vulgare)*				●			●	●
Oxford Ragwort *(Senecio squalidus)*		●		●	●		●	●
Pellitory-of-the-wall *(Parietaria judaica)*				●				
Pineapple Weed *(Matricaria matricarioides)*				●			●	●
Pink Sorrel *(Oxalis articulata)*				●	●			
Potamagetons *(Potamageton agg.)*		●				●	●	
Primrose *(Primula vulgaris)*	●	●		●		●		●
Purging Buckthorn *(Rhamus cathartica)*	●				●			
Purple Glasswort *(Salicornia ramosissima)*			●					
Purple Moor-grass *(Molinia caerulea)*								●
Pyramidal Orchid *(Anacamptis pyramidalis)*				●				

1. Woodland
2. Marshland
3. Estuary
4. Towns and Villages
5. Coast and Seashore
6. Inland Freshwater
7. Farmland
8. Heathland

SPECIES LIST	HABITATS							
1. Plants (continued)	1	2	3	4	5	6	7	8
Reed Sweet-grass *(Glyceria maxima)*		●						
Rose Campion *(Lychnis coronaria)*				●	●			
Rye Grass *(Lolium perenne)*	●	●	●	●	●	●	●	●
Saltwort *(Salsola kali)*					●			
Sea Beet *(Beta vulgaris ssp.maritima)*			●		●			
Sea Bindweed *(Convolvulus soldanella)*				●	●			
Sea Holly *(Eryngium maritimum)*					●			
Sea Lavender *(Limonium vulgare)*			●					
Sea Milkwort *(Glaux maritima)*			●					
Sea Purslane *(Halimione portulacoides)*			●					
Sea Rocket *(Cakile maritima)*					●			
Sea Sandwort *(Honckenya peploides)*					●			
Sheep's Fescue *(Festuca ovina)*				●				●
Sheep's Sorrel *(Rumex acetosella)*				●			●	●
Sheepsbit *(Jasione montana)*					●			
Silverweed *(Potentilla anserina)*		●				●		●
Smooth Sowthistle *(Sonchus oleraceus)*				●			●	●
Snap Dragon *(Antirrhinum majus)*				●	●			
Snow-in-summer *(Cerastium tomentosum)*				●	●			
Spring Beauty *(Claytonia perfoliata)*								●
Stinking Iris *(Iris foetidissima)*	●		●					
Sweet Alison *(Lobularia maritima)*				●	●			
Tormentil *(Potentilla erecta)*		●				●		●
Tufted Sedge *(Carex elata)*		●				●		
Tufted Vetch *(Vicia cracca)*	●			●			●	●
Water Crowfoot *(Ranunculus sp)*		●				●		
Water Dock *(Rumex hydrolapathum)*		●				●		
Water Fern *(Azolla filiculoides)*		●				●		
Water Plantain *(Alisma plantago-aquatica)*		●				●		
Water Violet *(Hottonia palustris)*		●				●		
Wavy Hair-grass *(Deschampsia flexuosa)*								●
Watercress *(Nasturtium officinale)*		●						
White Stonecrop *(Sedum alba)*				●	●		●	●

PART 3 ALPHABETICAL INDEX OF SPECIES AND THEIR HABITATS   95

1. Woodland
2. Marshland
3. Estuary
4. Towns and Villages
5. Coast and Seashore
6. Inland Freshwater
7. Farmland
8. Heathland

SPECIES LIST	HABITATS							
1. Plants (continued)	1	2	3	4	5	6	7	8
White Water Lily (Nymphaea alba)		●				●		
Wild Angelica (Angelica sylvestris)		●				●		
Wood Sage (Teucrium scorodonia)		●					●	
Woolly Hawkweed (Hieracium lanatum)				●				
Yellow Corydalis (Pseudofumaria lutea)				●				
Yellow Flag Iris (Iris pseudacorus)		●				●		
Yellow Loosestrife (Lysimachia vulgaris)		●				●		
Yellow Rattle (Rhinanthus minor)		●			●			●
Yellow Water Lily (Nuphar lutea)		●				●		
Yorkshire Fog (Holcus lanatus)	●	●	●	●	●	●	●	●

2. Trees and Shrubs	1	2	3	4	5	6	7	8
Alder (Alnus glutinosa)	●	●		●		●		
Ash (Fraxinus excelsior)	●							
Beech (Fagus sylvatica)	●							
Blackthorn (Prunus spinosa)							●	
Bramble (Rubus fruticosus agg.)							●	
Cherry Plum (Prunus cerasifera)							●	
Crab Apple (Malus sylvestris)	●							
Crack Willow (Salix fragilis)		●						
Cricket Bat Willow (Salix alba var. caerulea)		●						
Dogwood (Cornus sanguinea)							●	
Elder (Sambucus nigra)							●	
English Yew (Taxus baccata)	●							
Field Maple (Acer campestre)							●	
Gorse (Ulex europaeus)								●
Grey Poplar (Populus canescens)				●				
Hawthorn (Crataegus monogyna)				●			●	●
Hazel (Corylus avellana)							●	
Holm Oak (Quercus ilex)	●							
Hornbeam (Carpinus betulus)	●							
Horse Chestnut (Aesculus hippocastanum)	●							

1. Woodland
2. Marshland
3. Estuary
4. Towns and Villages
5. Coast and Seashore
6. Inland Freshwater
7. Farmland
8. Heathland

SPECIES LIST	HABITATS							
2. Trees and Shrubs (continued)	1	2	3	4	5	6	7	8
Irish Yew (Taxus fastigiata)	●							
Ling (Calluna vulgaris)								●
London Plane (Platanus x hybrida)				●				
Oregon Grape (Mahonia aquifolium)	●							
Pedunculate Oak (Quercus robur)	●							
Rhododendron (Rhododendron ponticum)							●	
Rowan (Sorbus aucuparia)	●							
Scots Pine (Pinus sylvestris)	●							
Sessile Oak (Quercus petrea)	●							
Silver Birch (Betula pendula)	●							
Small-leaved Elm (Ulmus SSp. minor)	●							
Spindle (Euonymus europaeus)							●	
Sweet Chestnut (Castanea sativa)	●							
White Birch (Betula pubescens)	●							
White Poplar (Populus alba)				●				
White Willow (Salix alba)		●						

3. Birds	1	2	3	4	5	6	7	8
Arctic Skua					●			
Arctic Tern			●		●	●		
Artic Warbler	●							
Avocet		●	●			●		
Balearic Shearwater					●			
Barn Owl			●		●	●		
Barnacle Goose			●	●				
Barred Warbler					●			●
Bar-tailed Godwit			●	●				
Bearded Tit			●			●		
Bewick's Swan			●	●				
Bittern			●			●		
Black Redstart					●	●		
Black Stork	●	●				●		
Black Tern			●			●		

PART 3 ALPHABETICAL INDEX OF SPECIES AND THEIR HABITATS

1. Woodland
2. Marshland
3. Estuary
4. Towns and Villages
5. Coast and Seashore
6. Inland Freshwater
7. Farmland
8. Heathland

SPECIES LIST	HABITATS							
3. Birds (continued)	1	2	3	4	5	6	7	8
Blackbird	●			●			●	
Blackcap	●			●				
Black-headed Gull		●	●	●	●	●		
Black-necked Grebe			●		●	●		
Black-tailed Godwit		●	●					
Black-winged Stilt		●	●					
Blue Tit	●			●			●	●
Bonelli's Warbler	●							
Brambling	●			●			●	●
Brent Goose		●	●		●			
Broad-billed Sandpiper		●	●					
Bullfinch	●						●	
Canada Goose		●	●			●		
Carrion Crow	●	●		●			●	
Caspian Tern			●		●	●		
Cetti's Warbler						●		
Chaffinch	●			●			●	●
Chiffchaff	●			●			●	
Coal Tit	●			●				
Collared Dove				●			●	
Common Buzzard	●	●					●	●
Common Eider					●			
Common Gull		●	●	●	●	●	●	
Common Redstart	●			●				●
Common Sandpiper		●	●		●	●		
Common Scoter					●			
Common Snipe		●	●			●		
Common Tern		●	●		●	●		
Common Whitethroat				●			●	●
Coot		●	●			●		
Cormorant	●	●	●		●	●		
Corn Bunting		●					●	
Corncrake							●	

1. Woodland
2. Marshland
3. Estuary
4. Towns and Villages
5. Coast and Seashore
6. Inland Freshwater
7. Farmland
8. Heathland

SPECIES LIST	HABITATS							
3. Birds (continued)	1	2	3	4	5	6	7	8
Crossbill	●							
Cuckoo	●			●			●	●
Curlew		●	●			●	●	
Curlew Sandpiper		●	●					
Dartford Warbler							●	●
Dunlin		●	●		●			
Dunnock	●			●			●	●
Egyptian Goose		●	●			●		
Fieldfare	●	●		●			●	●
Firecrest	●			●				
Fulmar					●			
Gadwall		●	●			●		
Garden Warbler	●			●				
Garganey		●				●		
Glaucous Gull			●		●			
Goldcrest	●			●				
Golden Oriole	●							
Golden Plover		●	●				●	
Goldeneye			●		●	●		
Goldfinch	●	●		●			●	●
Goosander			●			●		
Grasshopper Warbler		●				●		
Great Black-backed Gull			●	●	●	●		
Great Crested Grebe			●		●	●		
Great Skua					●			
Great Spotted Woodpecker	●			●				
Great Tit	●			●			●	●
Greater Sand Plover			●					
Greater Yellowlegs			●					
Green Woodpecker	●			●				
Greenfinch	●	●		●			●	
Greenshank		●	●					
Grey Heron	●	●	●			●		

PART 3 ALPHABETICAL INDEX OF SPECIES AND THEIR HABITATS

1. Woodland
2. Marshland
3. Estuary
4. Towns and Villages
5. Coast and Seashore
6. Inland Freshwater
7. Farmland
8. Heathland

SPECIES LIST	HABITATS							
3. Birds (continued)	1	2	3	4	5	6	7	8
Grey Partridge		●					●	
Grey Phalarope				●		●		
Grey Plover				●				
Greylag Goose		●	●			●		
Guillemot					●			
Gull-billed Tern			●		●			
Hawfinch	●							
Hen Harrier		●						●
Herring Gull		●	●	●	●	●	●	
Hobby	●						●	●
Hoopoe	●						●	
House Martin				●				
House Sparrow				●			●	
Iceland Gull			●		●			
Icterine Warbler	●							
Jack Snipe		●						
Jackdaw	●	●		●			●	
Jay	●			●			●	
Kentish Plover			●		●			
Kestrel	●	●		●			●	●
Kingfisher		●	●			●		
Kittiwake					●			
Knot			●		●			
Lapland Bunting		●			●			
Lapwing		●	●				●	
Leach's Petrel					●			
Lesser Black-backed Gull		●	●	●	●	●		
Lesser Spotted Woodpecker	●							
Lesser Whitethroat	●			●			●	●
Linnet		●		●			●	●
Little Auk					●			
Little Egret		●	●			●		
Little Grebe		●	●			●		

1. Woodland
2. Marshland
3. Estuary
4. Towns and Villages
5. Coast and Seashore
6. Inland Freshwater
7. Farmland
8. Heathland

SPECIES LIST	HABITATS							
3. Birds (continued)	1	2	3	4	5	6	7	8
Little Gull			●		●			
Little Owl	●						●	
Little Ringer Plover		●				●		
Little Stint		●	●		●			
Little Tern			●		●	●		
Long-eared Owl	●							
Long-tailed Duck					●			
Long-tailed Tit	●			●				
Magpie	●	●		●			●	●
Mallard		●	●			●		
Manx Shearwater					●			
Marsh Harrier		●				●		
Marsh Tit	●							
Meadow Pipit		●					●	●
Mediterranean Gull			●		●			
Merlin		●	●				●	●
Moorhen		●		●		●		
Mute Swan		●	●			●		
Nightingale	●							●
Nightjar	●							●
Nuthatch	●							
Osprey			●		●	●		
Oystercatcher		●	●		●		●	
Pallas's Warbler	●							●
Pectoral Sandpiper		●	●					
Peregrine		●	●		●			
Pheasant	●						●	●
Pied Flycatcher	●			●				
Pied Wagtail		●		●			●	
Pine Bunting							●	
Pink Footed Goose		●	●			●	●	
Pintail		●	●			●		
Pochard		●	●			●		

PART 3 ALPHABETICAL INDEX OF SPECIES AND THEIR HABITATS

1. Woodland
2. Marshland
3. Estuary
4. Towns and Villages
5. Coast and Seashore
6. Inland Freshwater
7. Farmland
8. Heathland

SPECIES LIST	HABITATS							
3. Birds (continued)	1	2	3	4	5	6	7	8
Purple Sandpiper					●			
Quail							●	
Razorbill					●			
Red Kite	●						●	●
Red-backed Shrike								●
Red-breasted Merganser			●		●	●		
Red-flanked Bluetail	●			●				
Red-legged Partridge		●		●			●	●
Red-necked Grebe			●		●			
Red-necked Phalarope			●		●	●		
Redpoll	●							●
Redshank		●	●					
Red-throated Diver			●		●			
Redwing	●	●		●			●	
Reed Bunting		●				●		
Reed Warbler		●				●		
Ring Ouzel		●					●	●
Ringed Plover		●	●		●			
Robin	●			●			●	●
Rock Pipit			●		●			
Rook	●	●		●			●	●
Roseate Tern			●		●			
Ruddy Duck						●		
Ruff		●	●			●		
Sabine's Gull					●			
Sand Martin					●	●		
Sanderling			●		●			
Sandwich Tern			●		●			
Scaup			●		●	●		
Sedge Warbler		●				●		
Shelduck		●	●		●	●		
Shore Lark			●		●			
Short-eared Owl		●						

1. Woodland
2. Marshland
3. Estuary
4. Towns and Villages
5. Coast and Seashore
6. Inland Freshwater
7. Farmland
8. Heathland

SPECIES LIST	HABITATS							
3. Birds (continued)	1	2	3	4	5	6	7	8
Shoveler		●	●			●		
Siskin	●			●				
Skylark		●			●		●	
Slavonian Grebe			●		●	●		
Smew			●			●		
Snow Bunting		●			●			
Song Thrush	●			●			●	
Sooty Shearwater					●			
Sparrow Hawk	●			●			●	●
Spoonbill		●	●					
Spotted Flycatcher	●			●				
Spotted Redshank		●	●					
Starling	●	●		●			●	
Stock Dove	●	●		●			●	
Stonechat		●						●
Storm Petrel					●			
Swallow		●		●			●	
Swift				●		●		
Tawny Owl	●			●				
Teal		●	●			●		
Temminck's Stint		●	●					
Treecreeper	●							
Tufted Duck		●	●			●		
Turnstone			●		●			
Turtle Dove	●						●	●
Twite		●	●		●			
Velvet Scoter					●			
Water Rail		●				●		
Waxwing				●				
Wheatear		●			●			●
Whimbrel		●	●					
Whinchat		●					●	●
White Stork		●						

PART 3 ALPHABETICAL INDEX OF SPECIES AND THEIR HABITATS

1. Woodland
2. Marshland
3. Estuary
4. Towns and Villages
5. Coast and Seashore
6. Inland Freshwater
7. Farmland
8. Heathland

SPECIES LIST	\multicolumn{8}{c	}{HABITATS}
3. Birds (continued)	1	2	3	4	5	6	7	8
White-fronted Goose		●	●					
White-rumped Sandpiper			●					
White-winged Black Tern		●	●			●		
Whooper Swan		●	●			●		
Wigeon		●	●		●			
Willow Tit	●							
Willow Warbler	●			●				
Wood Warbler	●							
Woodcock	●						●	●
Woodlark	●							●
Woodpigeon	●	●		●			●	
Wren	●			●				
Wryneck	●						●	
Yellow-browed Warbler	●							
Yellow Hammer		●					●	●
Yellow-legged Gull			●		●			

4. Mammals	1	2	3	4	5	6	7	8
Bank Vole (Clethrionomys glareolus)		●					●	
Brown Hare (Lepus capensis)		●		●			●	●
Brown Rat (Rattus norvegicus)		●		●		●	●	●
Chinese Water Deer (Hydropotes inermis)		●				●	●	●
Common Field Vole (Microtus agrestis)		●					●	●
Common Seal (Phoca vitulina)			●		●			
Coypu (Myocaster coypus)		●				●		
Grey Seal (Halychoerus grypus)			●		●			
Grey Squirrel (Sciurus carolinensis)	●	●		●			●	●
Harvest Mouse (Micromys minutus)							●	
Hedgehog (Erinaceus europaeus)	●	●		●			●	●
House Mouse (Mus domesticus)	●			●			●	●
Mink (Mustela vison)	●	●				●		
Mole (Talpa europaea)	●	●		●			●	●
Muntjac Deer (Muntiacus reevesi)	●			●		●		●

1. Woodland
2. Marshland
3. Estuary
4. Towns and Villages
5. Coast and Seashore
6. Inland Freshwater
7. Farmland
8. Heathland

SPECIES LIST	HABITATS							
4. Mammals (continued)	1	2	3	4	5	6	7	8
Noctule Bat (Nyctalus noctula)	●			●		●		
Otter (Lutra lutra)		●		●		●		
Pipistrelle Bat (Pipistrellus pipistrellus)	●	●		●		●	●	●
Rabbit (Oryctolagus cuniculus)	●	●	●	●		●	●	●
Red Deer (Cervus elephas)	●						●	
Red Fox (Vulpes vulpes)	●	●	●	●	●	●	●	●
Stoat (Mustela erminea)	●	●				●	●	●
Water Shrew (Neomys fodiens)		●				●		
Weasel (Mustela nivalis)	●	●	●	●		●	●	●
Wood Mouse (Apodemus sylvaticus)	●			●			●	●

5. Insects - Butterflies	1	2	3	4	5	6	7	8
Brimstone (Gonepteryx rhamni)	●	●	●	●		●	●	●
Brown Argus (Aricia agestis)						●		●
Camberwell Beauty (Nymphalis antiopa)				●				
Comma (Polygonia c-album)	●	●		●		●	●	●
Common Blue (polyommatus icarus)		●	●	●	●	●	●	●
Dark-green Fritillary (Mesoacidalia aglaja)				●				
Essex Skipper (Thymelicus lineola)	●	●		●		●	●	●
Gatekeeper (Pyronia tithonus)		●		●		●	●	●
Grayling (Hipparchia semele)		●			●			
Green-veined White (Artogeia napi)	●	●	●	●		●	●	●
Holly Blue (Celastrina argiolus)	●	●		●			●	●
Large Skipper (Ochlodes venatus)	●	●			●		●	●
Large White (Pieris brassicae)	●	●	●	●	●	●	●	●
Meadow Brown (Maniola jurtina)		●		●			●	
Orange Tip (Anthocharis cardamines)		●				●		
Peacock (Inachis io)	●	●	●	●		●	●	●
Painted Lady (cynthia cardui)	●	●	●	●		●	●	●
Purple Hairstreak (Quercusia quercus)	●							●
Red Admiral (Vanessa atlanta)	●	●	●	●	●	●	●	●
Ringlet (Aphantopus hyperantus)	●							●
Small Copper (Lycaena phlaeas)		●					●	●

PART 3 ALPHABETICAL INDEX OF SPECIES AND THEIR HABITATS   105

1. Woodland
2. Marshland
3. Estuary
4. Towns and Villages
5. Coast and Seashore
6. Inland Freshwater
7. Farmland
8. Heathland

| SPECIES LIST | HABITATS ||||||||
5. Insects (continued) - Butterflies	1	2	3	4	5	6	7	8
Small Heath (Coenonympha pamphilus)								●
Small Skipper (Thymelicus flavus)		●			●			●
Small Tortoiseshell (Aglais urticae)	●	●	●	●	●	●	●	●
Small White (Artogeia rapae)	●	●	●	●	●	●	●	●
Speckled Wood (Parage aegaria)	●							
Swallowtail (Papilio machaon)		●				●		
Wall Brown (Lasiommata megera)							●	●
White Admiral (Ladoga camilla)	●							●

5. Insects (continued) - Moths	1	2	3	4	5	6	7	8
Black Arches (Lymantria monacha)	●							●
Blackneck (Lygephila pastinum)		●				●		
Bordered White (Bupalus piniaria)	●							
Broad-bordered Bee Hawk-moth (Hemaris fuciformis)	●							●
Buff-tip (Phalera bucephala)	●				●		●	●
Cinnabar (Tyria jacobaea)		●						●
Clouded Border (Lomaspilis marginata)	●	●					●	●
Common Forrester (Adscita statices)								●
Common Heath (Ematurga atomaria)								●
Cream-spot Tiger Moth (Arctia villica)	●							●
Five-spot Burnet (Zygaena trifolii)		●						●
Grey Dagger (Acronicta psi)	●	●		●			●	●
Latticed Heath (Semiothosa clathrata)		●						●
Lime Hawk-moth (Mimas tiliae)	●			●				
Longhorn Moth (Nemophora degeerella)		●				●		●
Magpie Moth (Abraxus grossulariata)				●			●	●
Merveille-du-jour (Dichonia aprilina)	●			●				●
Micro-moth (Adela reaumurella)	●			●				●
Muslin Moth (Diaphora mendica)	●							●
November Moth (Epirrita dilutata)	●			●				
Oak Eggar (Lasiocampa quercus)	●			●				●
Pebble Hook-tip (drepana falcataria)	●							
Pine Hawk-moth (Hyloicus pinastri)	●			●				

1. Woodland
2. Marshland
3. Estuary
4. Towns and Villages
5. Coast and Seashore
6. Inland Freshwater
7. Farmland
8. Heathland

SPECIES LIST	HABITATS							
5. Insects (continued) - Moths	1	2	3	4	5	6	7	8
Poplar Hawk-moth (Laothoe populi)	●			●				
Silver Y (Autographa gamma)	●	●	●	●	●	●	●	●
Sycamore (Acronicta aceris)	●			●			●	●
The Engrailed (Ectropis bistortata)	●			●				●
Vapourer (Orgyia antiqua)	●			●				●
White Wave (Cabera pusaria)	●	●		●				●

SPECIES LIST	HABITATS							
5. Insects (continued) - Dragonflies and Damselflies	1	2	3	4	5	6	7	8
Black Darter (Sympetrum danae)				●				●
Black-tailed Skimmer (Orthetrum cancellatum)		●				●		●
Broad-bodied Chaser (Libellula depressa)		●				●		●
Brown Hawker (Aeshna grandis)		●		●		●		●
Common Darter (Sympetrum striolatum)		●	●	●		●	●	●
Emperor Dragonfly (Anax imperator)		●				●		
Four-spotted Chaser (Libellula quadrimaculata)		●				●		●
Hairy Hawker (Brachytron pratense)		●				●		●
Migrant Hawker (Aeshna mixta)	●	●		●	●	●	●	●
Norfolk Hawker (Aeshna isosceles)		●				●		●
Ruddy Darter (Sympetrum sanguineum)		●	●	●		●	●	●
Scarce Chaser (Libellula fulva)		●				●		
Southern Hawker (Aeshna cyanea)		●		●		●	●	●
Vagrant Darter (Sympetrum vulgatum)				●	●			
Yellow-winged Darter (Sympetrum flaviolum)				●	●	●		
Azure Damselfly (Coenagrion puella)		●		●		●		
Banded Demoiselle (Calopteryx splendens)		●				●		
Blue-tailed Damselfly (Ischnura elegans)		●		●		●		
Common Blue Damselfly (Enallagma cyathigerum)		●		●		●		
Large Red Damselfly (Pyrrhosoma nymphula)		●		●		●		●
Red-eyed Damselfly (Erithromma najas)		●				●		
Variable Damselfly (Coenagrion pulchellum)		●				●		

PART 3 ALPHABETICAL INDEX OF SPECIES AND THEIR HABITATS 107

1. Woodland
2. Marshland
3. Estuary
4. Towns and Villages
5. Coast and Seashore
6. Inland Freshwater
7. Farmland
8. Heathland

SPECIES LIST	HABITATS							
5. Insects (continued) - Other Insects	1	2	3	4	5	6	7	8
Alder Fly (Sialis lutaria)		●	●			●		
Aphid (Adelges abietis)	●							
American Cockroach (Periplaneta Americana)				●				
Australian Cockroach (Periplaneta australasiae)				●				
Birch-leaf Roller (Depaurus betulae)	●	●				●	●	●
Braconid (Apanteles glomeratus)	●	●		●		●	●	●
Buff-tailed Bumble Bee (Bombus terrestris)	●	●		●		●	●	●
Cabbage Root Fly (Delia radicum)				●			●	
Caddis Fly (Anabolia nervosa)		●				●		●
Caddis Fly (Limnephilus flavicornis)		●				●		●
Click Beetle (Agriotes lineatus)	●	●		●		●	●	●
Coast Leaf-cutter Bee (Magachile maritima)	●	●		●	●		●	●
Colorado Beetle (Leptinotarsa decemlineata)							●	
Common Carder Bee (Bombus pascuorum)		●		●			●	
Common Cranefly (Tipula oleracea)	●	●	●	●	●	●	●	●
Common Earwig (Forficula auricularia)	●	●		●		●	●	
Common Flower Bug (Anthocoris nemorum)	●	●		●				●
Common Mayfly (Ephemera danica)		●				●		
Common Wasp (Vespula vulgaris)	●	●		●	●	●	●	●
Common Water Beetle (Acilius sulcatus)		●		●		●		
Cranefly (Tipula paludosa)	●	●	●	●	●		●	●
Cream-spot Ladybird (Calvia 14-guttata)	●						●	●
Cream-streaked Ladybird (Harmonia 4-punctata)	●							●
Devils Coach Horse (Staphylinus olens)	●	●		●		●	●	●
Dor Beetle (Geotrupes stercorarius)		●						
Drone Fly (Eristalis tenax)	●	●		●		●	●	●
Eyed Ladybird (Anatis ocellata)	●							●
Fish Louse (Argulus foliaceus)		●				●		
Forest Bug (Pentatoma rufipes)	●							●
Fourteen-spot Ladybird (Propylea 14-punctata)	●	●		●		●	●	●
Freshwater Shrimp (Gammarus pulex)		●				●		
Fur Beetle (Attagenus pellio)				●				
Gall-mite (Eriophyes macrorhynchus)	●			●			●	●

1. Woodland
2. Marshland
3. Estuary
4. Towns and Villages
5. Coast and Seashore
6. Inland Freshwater
7. Farmland
8. Heathland

SPECIES LIST	HABITATS							
5. Insects (continued) - Other Insects	1	2	3	4	5	6	7	8
Gall-mite *(Eriophyes marginatus)*	●	●		●		●		
Gall-wasp *(Andricus quercuscalicis)*	●			●			●	●
Gall-wasp *(Biorhiza pallida)*	●						●	●
Gall-wasp *(Diplolepsis rosae)*	●	●		●		●	●	●
Gall-wasp *(Neuroterus albipes)*	●			●				●
Gall-wasp *(Neuroterus numismalis)*	●			●				●
Gall-wasp *(Neuroterus quercusbaccarum)*	●			●				●
Great Diving Beetle *(Dytiscus marginalis)*		●		●		●		●
Green Lacewing *(Chrysopa perla)*	●			●			●	●
Green Tiger Beetle *(Cicindela campestris)*								●
Hawthorn Shieldbug *(Acanthosoma haemorrhoidale)*	●						●	●
Holly Leaf-miner *(Phytomyza ilicis)*	●			●		●	●	●
Honey Bee *(Apis mellifera)*	●			●			●	●
Hoverfly *(Episyrphus balteatus)*	●	●		●		●	●	●
Hoverfly *(Heliophilus pendula)*	●	●		●		●	●	●
Hoverfly *(Scaeva pyrastri)*	●			●				●
Hoverfly *(Syrphus ribesii)*	●	●		●	●	●	●	●
Hoverfly *(Syrphus vitripennis)*	●	●		●	●	●	●	●
Hoverfly *(Volucella pelluscens)*	●			●				●
Ichneumon *(Rhyssa persuasoria)*	●							●
Large Caddis Fly *(Phryganea grandis)*		●				●		
Large Cranefly *(Tipula maxima)*		●				●		
Lesser Water Boatman *(Corixa lacustris)*		●				●		
Longhorn Beetle *(Agapanthea vilosoviridescens)*		●				●		●
Longhorn Beetle *(Strangalia maculata)*	●	●		●			●	
Parent Bug *(Elasmucha grisea)*	●							●
Pine Ladybird *(Exochomus 4-pustulatus)*	●							●
Pond Skater *(Gerris lacustris)*		●		●		●		
Praying Mantis *(Mantis religiosa)*				●				
Red Osmia *(Osmia rufa)*	●			●				
Red Wasp *(Vespula rufa)*	●			●				●
Red Weevil *(Attelabus nitens)*	●							●
Red-banded Sand Wasp *(Amophila sabulosa)*					●			●

PART 3   ALPHABETICAL INDEX OF SPECIES AND THEIR HABITATS   109

1. Woodland
2. Marshland
3. Estuary
4. Towns and Villages
5. Coast and Seashore
6. Inland Freshwater
7. Farmland
8. Heathland

SPECIES LIST	HABITATS								
5. Insects (continued) - Other Insects	1	2	3	4	5	6	7	8
Reed Beetle *(Donacia aquatica)*		●				●		
Saucer Bug *(Hyocoris cimicoides)*		●				●		
Sawfly *(Pontania proxima)*	●	●						●
Seven-spot Ladybird *(Coccinella 7-punctata)*	●	●	●	●	●	●	●	●
Tawny Mining Bee *(Andrena fulva)*				●				●
Tree Wasp *(Dolichovespula sylvestris)*	●			●			●	●
Two-spot Ladybird *(Adalia bipunctata)*	●	●	●	●	●	●	●	●
Varied Carpet Beetle *(Anthrenus verbasci)*				●				
Violet Ground Beetle *(Carabus violaceus)*	●	●		●			●	●
Water Boatman *(Notonecta glauca)*		●				●		
Water Cricket *(Velia caprai)*		●				●		
Water Ladybird *(Anisosticta 19-punctata)*		●				●		
Water Scorpion *(Nepa cinerea)*		●				●		
Water Slater *(Asellus aquaticus)*		●		●		●		
Water Stick Insect *(Ranatra linearis)*		●				●		
Whirlygig Beetle *(Gyrinus natator)*		●				●		

6. Spiders	1	2	3	4	5	6	7	8
Garden Spider *(Araneus diadematus)*	●	●		●			●	●
House Spider *(Tegenaria domestica)*				●		●		
Spider *(Araneus quadratus)*		●						●
Spider *(Drassodes lapidosus)*	●			●				●
Spider *(Dysdera crocata)*	●			●			●	●
Spider *(Tetragantha extensa)*		●			●			
Spider *(Tibellus oblongus)*		●			●			
Water Spider *(Argyroneta aquatica)*		●				●		

7. Reptiles and Amphibians	1	2	3	4	5	6	7	8
Adder *(Vipera beris)*		●			●			●
Common Frog *(Rana temporaria)*		●		●		●	●	
Common Lizard *(Lacerta vivipara)*	●	●						●
Common Newt *(Triturus vulgaris)*		●		●		●	●	●

1. Woodland
2. Marshland
3. Estuary
4. Towns and Villages
5. Coast and Seashore
6. Inland Freshwater
7. Farmland
8. Heathland

SPECIES LIST	HABITATS							
5. Reptiles and Amphibians (continued)	1	2	3	4	5	6	7	8
Common Toad *(Bufo bufo)*		•		•		•		
Crested Newt *(Triturus cristatus)*						•		
Grass Snake *(Natrix natrix)*	•	•				•		•
Natterjack Toad *(Bufo calamita)*					•			•
Slow Worm *(Anguis fragilis)*	•			•		•	•	•

SPECIES LIST	HABITATS							
8. Fishes	1	2	3	4	5	6	7	8
Bass *(Dicentrarchus labrax)*			•	•				
Cod *(Gadus morhua)*			•	•				
Common Bream *(Abramis brama)*		•				•		
Common Carp *(Cyprinus carpio)*		•				•		
Common Eel *(Anguilla vulgaris)*			•		•	•		
Dab *(Limanda limanda)*					•			
Dace *(Leuciscus leuciscus)*						•		
Flounder *(Platichthys flesus)*			•		•			
Gudgeon *(Gobio gobio)*						•		
Lesser Weaver *(Echiichthys vipera)*					•			
Perch *(Perca fluviatilis)*		•				•		
Pike *(Esox lucius)*		•	•			•		
Roach *(Rutilus rutilus)*		•				•		
Rudd *(Scardinius erythrophthalmus)*		•				•		
Smelt *(Osmerus eperlanus)*			•					
Sole *(Solea solea)*					•			
Tench *(Tinca tinca)*		•				•		
Three-spined Stickleback *(Gasterosteus aculeatus)*		•				•		
Whiting *(Merlangius merlangus)*					•			

9. Fungi	1	2	3	4	5	6	7	8
Artist's Fungus *(Ganoderma applanatum)*	•			•				•
Beechwood Sickener *(Russula mairei)*	•							
Beef-steak Fungus *(Fistulina hepatica)*	•							
Birch Polypore *(Piptoporus betulinus)*	•			•			•	•

PART 3 ALPHABETICAL INDEX OF SPECIES AND THEIR HABITATS 111

1. Woodland
2. Marshland
3. Estuary
4. Towns and Villages
5. Coast and Seashore
6. Inland Freshwater
7. Farmland
8. Heathland

SPECIES LIST	HABITATS							
9. Fungi (continued)	1	2	3	4	5	6	7	8
Common Earthball *(Scleroderma citrinum)*	●			●				●
Common Puffball *(Lycoperdon echinatum)*	●							●
Death Cap *(Amanita phalloides)*	●							●
Fairy Ring *(Marasmius oreades)*	●	●		●			●	●
False Chanterelle *(Hygrophoropsis aurantiaca)*	●							
Fly Agaric *(Amanita muscaria)*	●							
Funnel Cap *(Clitocybe infundibuliformis)*	●							●
Liberty Cap *(Psilocybe semilanceata)*	●							●
No Common Name *(Lycoperdon foetidum)*	●							●
No Common Name *(Mycena filopes)*	●							●
No Common Name *(Mycena galopus)*	●							●
No Common Name *(Mycena sanguinolenta)*	●							●
Rufous Milk-cap *(Lactarius rufa)*	●							
Slippery Jack *(Suillus luteus)*	●							
Spotted Tough-shank *(Collybia maculata)*	●							●
Stinkhorn *(Phallus impudicus)*	●			●			●	●
Sulphur Tuft *(Hypholoma fasciculare)*	●							●
The Deceiver *(Laccaria laccata)*	●							●
The Sickener *(Russula emetica)*	●							
Wood Mushroom *(Agaricus silvicola)*	●							
Yellow Russula *(Russula ochroleuca)*	●							

List of Photographs

James Paget	(1)
Arthur Patterson and a young Ted Ellis	(2)
H. E. Hurrell at Microscope	(3)
P. E. Rumblelow	(4)
Typical Woodland Habitat	(5)
Spotted Flycatcher	(6)
Grey Squirrel	(7)
Primrose	(8)
Coppiced Hazel	(9)
Scots Pine	(10)
Longhorned Beetle *Strangalia maculata*	(11)
Stinkhorn Fungus	(12)
Sparrowhawk with prey	(13)
Brimstone on Thistle	(14)
Artichoke gall on Oak	(15)
Marble gall on Oak	(16)
Knopper gall on Oak	(17)
Nail gall on Large-leaved Lime	(18)
White Admiral Butterfly	(19)
Hawthorn Berries	(20)
Typical Marshland Habitat	(21)
Grey Heron	(22)
Sea Milkwort	(23)
Spider *Tetragantha extensa*	(24)
Swallowtail Butterfly	(25)
Norfolk Hawker	(26)
Grass Snake	(27)
Marsh Marigold	(28)
Hairy Hawker	(29)
Sunset on Breydon Water	(30)
Avocet	(31)
Common Scurvygrass	(32)
A View of Breydon from the Air	(33)
Berney Windpump	(34)
Typical Town Habitat - Yarmouth Cemetery	(35)
Typical Town Habitat - From St. Nicholas Church Tower	(36)
Song Thrush	(37)
Red Fox	(38)
Lesser Celandine	(39)
Canadian Fleabane	(40)
Hedgehog	(41)
Wasps' Nest in House Rafters	(42)

Peacock Butterfly	(43)
Magpie Moth	(44)
Garden Spider	(45)
Yellow-winged Darter	(46)
North Beach S.P.A. from the Air	(47)
The North Beach S.P.A in Early Summer	(48)
Common Eider Adult Drake	(49)
Grey Hair Grass	(50)
Dark-green Fritillary Butterflies	(51)
Seals on Scroby Sand	(52)
Typical Inland Freshwater Habitat - Lound Water	(53)
Great Crested Grebe	(54)
Mute Swan with Cygnets	(55)
Migrant Hawker	(56)
Common Frog	(57)
Four-spotted Chaser	(58)
Common Mayfly	(59)
Unbranched Burr Reed	(60)
White Water-lily	(61)
Water Dock	(62)
Alder Catkins	(63)
Typical Farmland Habitat	(64)
Hawthorn in Flower	(65)
Brown Hare	(66)
Fieldfare	(67)
Tawny Mining Bee	(69)
Bee Orchid	(70)
Green-veined White Butterfly	(71)
Typical Heathland Habitat - Belton Common	(72)
Silver Birch Showing the Witches Broom Gall	(73)
Spring Beauty	(74)
Wall Brown Butterfly	(75)
Yellowhammer	(76)
Grey-dagger Moth	(77)
Caterpillar of Grey-dagger Moth	(78)
Fly Agaric	(79)
Birch Polypore	(80)
Comma Butterfly	(81)
Natterjack Toad	(82)
Adder	(83)
Great Grey Slug	(84)
Large Black Slug	(85)
Garden Snails	(86)
Michael Seago	(87)

Suggested Further Reading

This list is intended as an introduction to the literature available. Some titles are regrettably out of print but may be obtained from your local library.

There are now many colourful guides to tempt the budding naturalist; some are better than others. Generally the "Collins" field guides have maintained a very high standard of presentation and information over the years and can be recommended.

There are also many learned and comprehensive books on every aspect of natural history; these have been excluded from this list as they are both specialist and expensive. However the Great Yarmouth Naturalists' Society includes members with special interests who will be pleased to help.

PLANTS, TREES AND SHRUBS

Beckett, Gillian and others. A Flora of Norfolk. G. Beckett 1999

Rose, Francis. The Wild Flower Key. Penguin Books 1981 (Re-issued 1991)

Hancy, Rex. The Study of Plant Galls in Norfolk. Norfolk and Norwich Naturalists' Society 1999

Mitchell, Alan and Wilkinson, John. The Trees of Britain and Northern Europe. Collins. 1988

BIRDS

Allard, Peter R. The Birds of Great Yarmouth. Norfolk and Norwich Naturalists' Society. 1990

Jonsson, Lars. Birds of Europe with North Africa and The Middle East. Christopher Helm. 1996

Taylor, Moss and others. The Birds of Norfolk. Pica Press. 1999

MAMMALS

Corbet, Gordon and Ovenden, Denys. The Mammals of Britain and Europe. Collins. 1980

INSECTS

Brooks, Margaret. Complete Guide to British Moths. Jonathan Cape. 1991

Brooks, Steve and Lewington, Richard. A Field Guide to the Dragonflies and Damselflies of Great Britain and Ireland. British Wildlife Publishing. 1997

Chinery, Michael. Field Guide to the Insects of Britain and Northern Europe third edition. Collins. 1993

Tolman, Tom and Lewington, Richard. Butterflies of Britain and Europe. (Collins Field Guide) Collins. 1997

SPIDERS

Roberts, Michael J. Spiders of Britain and Northern Europe. (Collins Field Guide). Collins. 1995

REPTILES AND AMPHIBIANS

Arnold, E. N and Burton, J. A. A Field Guide to the Reptiles and Amphibians of Gt. Britain and Europe. Collins. 1978

FISHES

Fitter, Richard and Manuel, Richard. Field Guide to the Freshwater Life of Britain and North-West Europe. Collins. 1986

Maitland, Peter S. Guide to the Freshwater Fish of Britain and Europe. revised edition Hamlyn 2000

FUNGI

Jordan, Michael. Encyclopaedia of Fungi of Britain and Europe. David and Charles. 1995

GENERAL

Paget, C. J. and Paget, James. Sketch of the Natural History of Yarmouth and its Neighbourhood. Longman, Rees and Co. 1834

Patterson, Arthur H. Nature in Eastern Norfolk. Methuen. 1905

Acknowledgements

We wish to gratefully acknowledge the help given to us from outside our Society. There have been many sources of help from both individuals, by way of wildlife records, and organisations large and small with information and sponsorship.

In particular the authors would like to offer their sincere thanks to the following:

BP Amoco Exploration	For sponsorship for computer software
Birds Eye Walls Ltd.	For sponsorship toward coloured photographs
Dr. Roy Baker Keith Clarke Derek Howlett	For records of molluscs etc.
Great Yarmouth Bird Club	For various records and photographs
Pat Nicholls GYNS	For the line drawings
Garth Coupland	For records of spiders and molluscs
Ordnance Survey	For waiving fees for the use of map on front cover
Ian Mills	For supplying bird photographs
D. & L. Studios	For allowing the use of some slides
Norfolk & Norwich Naturalists' Society	For financial assistance from the Peat fund
Rondor Printing Company	Special thanks to all the team for help and advice
David Bellamy	For providing us with the foreword

In addition to the above, the authors would like to thank their respective wives for their tolerance and understanding of the endless hours spent in isolation at the computer and for the numerous meetings needed to produce this publication; special thanks to Pam for providing tea and coffee during those meetings.

The Authors

PETER ALLARD

Peter Allard has had a lifelong interest in birds and natural history. As a result of his 40 years of regular monthly Breydon Water bird-counts, the estuary now enjoys statutory protection through its dual status as a Special Protection Area and as a Ramsar Site.

Although well known for successfully identifying a succession of rarer birds at both Breydon Water and Winterton Dunes, the conservation of birds plays a vital part in his life. For several years he was assistant warden at Winteron Dunes N.N.R. and was instrumental in achieving permanent protection for Little Terns nesting on Yarmouth North beach. A very successful Common Tern breeding colony at Breydon is due, in part, to his persistent efforts over 24 years.

A past secretary of the Great Yarmouth Naturalists' Society he formed, with others, the Great Yarmouth Bird Club in 1989 and became its first secretary.

He is author of "The Birds of Great Yarmouth" (1990) and a senior author of the recently published "The Birds of Norfolk". A third published book dealt with local maritime history and others are planned including one on Breydon Water.

Since 1964 he has been assistant editor of the Norfolk Bird Report and was for several years Norfolk Bird Recorder. A licensed ringer since 1977, he is a regular contributor to several bird magazines.

MICHAEL BEAN

Michael Bean was born in Great Yarmouth and has lived here all of his life. His interest in wildlife was instilled by the programmes produced at the BBC Natural History Unit in the 1960's. However, it was by serving his "apprenticeship" in the company of an older generation of naturalists that he became aware of the riches of the natural world.

He was at one time a volunteer warden for Breydon Water Local Nature Reserve and sat on its Advisory and Management Committees in the 1980's as the representative of The Norfolk and Norwich Naturalists' Society. He has spent the years exploring the nature around eastern Norfolk, especially its birdlife, as well as the area' landscape and history.

TONY BROWN

Tony first delved into the wonders of nature as a youngster in and around the dykes on the marshes that now form the Harfrey's Industrial estate. In those days there was a large open expanse of marshland divided up into fields with the dykes forming the boundaries to each one with a five barred gate at the entrance.

The dykes held a certain fascination for youngsters who were inquisitive, and teemed with all kinds of smaller wildlife, some of which could easily be seen swimming in the water between the plants and aquatic weeds. A net swept through the water would produce even more to fire the interest of an enquiring mind, for there were frogs, toads and newts to be seen, tadpoles sometimes by the dozens and all kinds of beetles and bugs. Some of these made a noise when touched and some caused pain when they nipped the fingers. He utilised jam jars and glass containers of all sizes to contain the creatures to enable further study and help to develop more understanding of this world so new to him.

As he grew older his interest developed and embraced most aspects of this truly fascinating hobby, but as more and more time was spent working and raising a family there seemed to be less time to indulge himself. The interest however remained throughout the years and now that Tony's family have all grown up and flown the nest there seems a little more time.

Insects have always been a source of great wonderment to him and he has spent a great deal of time watching, collecting and studying their ways with probably most emphasis on Dragonflies and Butterflies.

These groups have given him enormous pleasure through the years but he has never lost his affection for all kinds of fresh water life and still occasionally fills his aquarium with creatures for study.

He was asked to consider taking the office of Hon. Secretary to the Great Yarmouth Naturalists' Society in 1990 and has held the post since. He has worked very hard on behalf of the Society throughout this period and if pushed would say that he has enjoyed every minute of it. The publication of this book is due largely to his persistence.

KEN RIVETT

It all started about a year before leaving school (they left school at the age of 14 in those days). Ken and his friends spent their after school hours playing and wandering the marshes around Caister. Little did he realise that all this was his introduction to becoming a naturalist. This all came to a stop in 1948 when Ken was called to do two years conscription in the R.A.F. After a while he joined the station dance orchestra and spent most of his service as a musician. After leaving the service he carried on working as a musician for a number of years which took up most of his time but soon his hobby turned to growing plants which re-awakened his interest in natural history which in turn lead to wild plants. Teaching himself botany he and his wife joined the Great Yarmouth Naturalists' Society and many more of the local groups. These included The Suffolk Wildlife Trust for which he became chairman of the Lowestoft Branch, Lowestoft Field Club, The Norfolk and Norwich Naturalists' Society where he served as a member of the Council, The Norfolk Wildlife Trust and of course the Botanical Society of the British Isles. The last few years have been spent with the Norfolk Flora Group helping in the recording of the New Norfolk Flora. His wild plant records, which number over 30,000 around the Great Yarmouth area have greatly helped the team in the publication of this book.

BRIAN WOODEN

Brian Wooden is the current Chairman of the Great Yarmouth Naturalists' Society. His boyhood interest in natural history was rekindled when he and his wife took up country walking as a hobby. Their desire to understand and know more about what they were seeing on these walks lead them to the Society and a major new adult interest opened up.

Brian is a keen member of the RSPB and works as a volunteer on the Little Tern project each summer.

He is very active in all aspects of the Society but makes no secret of the fact that it is the field trips and midweek summer walks that bring him the most enjoyment. His interest is less specialised than that of the other authors of this book, but his drive and enthusiasm has much encouraged his co-authors and he has contributed much in bringing this book to publication.

Notes

Notes

Use this table for recording your own sightings.

1. Woodland
2. Marshland
3. Estuary
4. Towns and Villages
5. Coast and Seashore
6. Inland Freshwater
7. Farmland
8. Heathland

SPECIES LIST	HABITATS							
	1	2	3	4	5	6	7	8

Use this table for recording your own sightings.

1. Woodland
2. Marshland
3. Estuary
4. Towns and Villages
5. Coast and Seashore
6. Inland Freshwater
7. Farmland
8. Heathland

SPECIES LIST	\multicolumn{8}{c	}{HABITATS}
	1	2	3	4	5	6	7	8